D1035210

MISGUIDED JUSTICE

JUSTICE

The War *on* Drugs *and the*
Incarceration *of* Black Women

Stephanie Bush-Baskette, JD, PhD

iUniverse, Inc.
New York   Bloomington

Copyright © 2010 by Stephanie Bush-Baskette, JD, PhD

All rights reserved. No part of this book may be used or reproduced by any means, graphic, electronic, or mechanical, including photocopying, recording, taping or by any information storage retrieval system without the written permission of the publisher except in the case of brief quotations embodied in critical articles and reviews.

iUniverse books may be ordered through booksellers or by contacting:

iUniverse
1663 Liberty Drive
Bloomington, IN 47403
www.iuniverse.com
1-800-Authors (1-800-288-4677)

Because of the dynamic nature of the Internet, any Web addresses or links contained in this book may have changed since publication and may no longer be valid. The views expressed in this work are solely those of the author and do not necessarily reflect the views of the publisher, and the publisher hereby disclaims any responsibility for them.

ISBN: 978-1-4502-1738-5 (sc)
ISBN: 978-1-4502-1740-8 (dj)
ISBN: 978-1-4502-1739-2 (ebook)

Printed in the United States of America

iUniverse rev. date: 04/07/2010

For the women on the inside

CONTENTS

PREFACE

In 1995 I read an article by Marc Mauer and Tracey Huling in which the authors reported that between 1986 and 1991 there had been an 828 percent increase in the number of black women who were incarcerated for drug offenses.[1] This statistic shocked me for two reasons: first, the magnitude of the increase, and second, the fact that I had never before heard or read about any relationship between black women and drug laws. As an attorney, former state legislator, and gubernatorial cabinet member, I was already quite familiar with how the enactment of laws and the implementation of public policy impact individuals and society in unexpected, unpredicted, and unpublicized ways; this one statistic, however, would direct me to the next path in my professional career. My goal in life had evolved over the years, informed and supported by various experiences, with the common theme being my desire to help people to empower themselves to improve their lives and society. As an attorney, I used my skills of advocacy to represent people in contract negotiations, trials, real estate transactions, and adoptions, to get them closer to where they wanted to be. As a state legislator, I had the opportunity to change some of the policies and laws that impacted individuals and society. One of the major policy changes I sponsored was the Family Leave Law. In 1988 President George H. W. Bush vetoed it at the federal level, but I was able to negotiate it through passage in New Jersey. Years later the federal government would use New Jersey as a test case to determine if the policy should be enacted nationwide—and it was.

I left the New Jersey state legislature to join Governor James Florio's cabinet

---

1   Mauer, Mark and Tracey Huling. 1995. *Young Black Americans and the Criminal Justice System: Five Years Later.* Washington, DC: The Sentencing Project.

as the state commissioner of the New Jersey Department of Community Affairs. In assuming that role, I was able to implement policies that were closely related to many of the bills I had sponsored and committees I had chaired or sat on while in the legislature. I also became more keenly aware of the relationships between policy, politics, bureaucracy, and power.

Prior to leaving public life, I became concerned about the absence of informed public participation in the legislative and public policy process. In 1990 as I advocated for raising the minimum wage in New Jersey to $5.05, I found that as a prime sponsor of the bill, I was one of just a handful of people present at a committee meeting to argue why this was important to working people in New Jersey. Business lobbyists retorted that there was no need to do so because, for example, they already paid their dishwashers $17.00 an hour. I also became intensely aware of the power the media had on the formation of public opinion. What was most disconcerting was that the media's influence was not just through newspaper articles that might have been written from sometimes biased and uninformed perspectives; equally influential were headlines, bumper stickers, billboards, and the ranting and raving performed by many talking heads on television "news" programs. I began to understand how important an active, informed public is to the development and implementation of good public policy. It is not about "government they"; it is more appropriately "government we." This recognition led me to earn a doctorate, as I determined that a very good place to transfer the tools by which people can empower themselves and society was at a university. It was my goal not to tell people *what* to think but *how* to think.

Now, years after teaching at a university, being a researcher for a national nonprofit research institute, and directing an academic research center that is tasked with bridging the research divide between community and campus, I realize that it is not simply about teaching people how to think; it is equally important to provide information that they can use in their personal and professional lives to make informed policy decisions. Thus, I share my experiences and expertise as a policy maker, lawyer, politician, educator, researcher, and person who believes that we all have a role to play in the development, implementation, and review of policies that impact our society.

This book is not about me, but as a researcher and author, I believe that it is important that the conveyor of information provide relevant background to readers that explains who she is and how she comes to the research. As human beings, we all have our perceptions of reality and something to share; all are important in the development of policy.

My purpose for writing this book is to provide information with which we may answer these questions: Shortly after its inception, was the war on drugs a war against black women? Now, more than twenty years later, as the general public and the media's focus on the war on drugs has diminished, do the drug policies continue to impact the incarceration of black women? If so, how?

When the initial drug laws were passed, there was no research available to support or refute the underlying assumptions of the bills that were being enacted. In the past twenty years, not only has research by which to evaluate the policies emerged, but there have also been various methods approved by which to circumvent the perceived harshness of the laws in specific situations. The question that must also be asked is: have these remedial alternatives (or "safety valves") lessened the harshness of the application of the drug laws on black women?

Once the reader has completed this volume, it is expected that he or she will understand some of the demands that led to the enactment of the original federal drug legislation, as well as the ensuing remedial alternatives; the political process that responded to the demands, including who the governmental actors and institutions were who played and continue to play an ongoing role in this policy development and analysis; the decisions and policies that resulted from the political process; the impacts the outcomes and policies have had on black women in the federal system, as well as an idea of who these women are; and how these outcomes have or may lead to new or continuing demands and support for further political involvement.[2]

Before most chapters, I have included a short description about an actual black woman who has been incarcerated in the federal system for a drug offense related to crack cocaine. I do so to continuously remind us that this discussion is about real human beings and is not a merely academic debate about policy, politics, and statistics. After reading each case, I suggest that you ask yourself: assuming the facts as presented are true, did the punishment this woman received fit the crime, or was it misguided justice?

---

2   See Figure1-1, *Urban Political Systems Model in Cities, Politics, and Public Policy*, edited by John P. Pelissero, Washington, DC: CQ Press, 2003: 4.

———ACKNOWLEDGMENTS———

This book took years of research and writing. I had many beings—both human and four-legged—who provided me with the support I needed to accomplish this goal. I especially want to thank my family: Ernest, who has always been supportive of my writing; my parents, who have cheered me on all of my life; and my critters, who provide me the environment I need in which to think and write. I give a very special thanks to Vivian Pacheco for all of her assistance.

CHAPTER ONE

Black Females and the War on Drugs:
The First Twenty Years

Alfreda R. – Ten Years for Conspiracy to Distribute Crack Cocaine[3]

At the time of her arrest, Alfreda was a high school guidance counselor. She had two master's degrees, her own home, and a car. She was a single parent of one son, David, who had begun selling drugs. Alfreda's only previous encounter with the law had been when she drove with a suspended license and was put on probation from DMV.

Due to her son's behavior, Alfreda put him out of her home, although she agreed to help him, as best she could on her salary, to get an apartment and a used car. David was arrested and called his mom for help. He told her that a friend owed him some money and asked her to call the friend's mother and ask for $4,500 so that he could hire an attorney. Alfreda called the friend's mother. The next morning, Alfreda's home was raided by law enforcement, and they found $4,500 of marked bills in her home safe. David had placed the money there without her knowledge.

Because she had made the telephone call to the friend's parent, Alfreda was charged as a conspirator. The friend became a government informant and received immunity for his testimony. Alfreda received a sentence of ten years for conspiracy to distribute crack cocaine, although there was no evidence presented that linked Alfreda to any drug activity.

---

3   *Human Rights* 95. Alfreda Robinson, Drug War POW. November 27, 2009. http://wwwhr95.org/robinson,a.htm.

Authorities seized her home, although she could prove it had been purchased legally with proceeds from a personal injury lawsuit.

Sentence: ten years for conspiracy to distribute crack cocaine

---

Black women suffered from the greatest increase in the percentage of inmates incarcerated for drug offenses in the 1980s and 1990s. Although Michael Tonry, a researcher and author of the book *Malign Neglect*, proposed that the drug policies of 1987–88 had led to the increased incarceration of black males who lived in the inner city, while having no positive impact on the drug problems in the United States[4], the question of the impact on black women remains virtually unanswered. It can easily be argued that the war on drugs is actually a war against the users and low-level dealers of crack cocaine because of the disproportional penalties attached to offenses that involve crack cocaine as compared to other forms of cocaine and other types of drugs. What does this mean as it relates to black women? At the state level, the number of black women who were incarcerated for drug offenses between 1986 and 1991 increased by 828 percent (Table 1.1). This increase was approximately twice that of black males (429 percent) and more than three times that of white females (241 percent).[5] Mark Mauer and Tracey Huling of the Sentencing Project also found that between 1980 and 1992, the number of black women in state or federal prisons for any offense increased by 278 percent while the number of black men increased by 186 percent. The overall prison population increased by 168 percent during that period.[6]

---

4   Tonry, 1995.
5   Mauer and Huling, 1995, 20.
6   Mauer and Huling, 1995, 19.

Table 1.1: State Prisoners Incarcerated for Drug Offenses by Race/Ethnic Origin and Sex, 1986 and 1991

Race	1986 Male	1986 Female	1991 Male	1991 Female	Percent Increase Male	Percent Increase Female
White, non-Hispanic	12,868	969	26,452	3,300	106%	241%
Black, non-Hispanic	13,974	667	73,932	6,193	429%	828%
Hispanic	8,484	664	35,965	2,843	324%	328%
Other	604	70	1,323	297	119%	324%
Total	**35,930**	**2,370**	**137,672**	**12,633**	**283%**	**433%**

Source: Mauer and Huling, *Young Black Americans and the Criminal Justice System*, 20.

Black women also had the greatest percentage of increase in the number of persons who were under the supervision of the criminal justice system—jail or prison, parole or probation—with a rate of increase of 72 percent between 1990 and 1996.[7]

At times black women even constituted a greater proportion of incarcerated females than the proportion of incarcerated males represented by black men. For example, in 1993 a total of 48,170 females were incarcerated in state correctional institutions. Of this group, black females comprised 51.1 percent (24,595), and white females constituted 43.9 percent (21,135) of the population of incarcerated females. Black males constituted 49.7 percent of the population of males in state prisons in 1993.[8] Similarly, the federal jurisdiction had a greater percentage of black females (39.1 percent) among incarcerated females than black males (33.22 percent) among incarcerated males.[9]

Considering that black females comprised about 12.8 percent of the general female population over the age of 18 and black males comprised about 11.2 percent of the general adult male population of the United States,[10] these

---

7   BJS, 1999, 4.
8   BJS, 1995.
9   U.S. Dept. of Justice, Bureau of Justice Statistics, "Correctional Populations in the United States, 1993." U.S. Census Bureau, "1990 Census."
10   U.S. Census, 2006. Black females comprise about 6.7 percent and black males about 5.4

data indicate that both groups have been represented disproportionately in the population of incarcerated individuals. These data show that the incarceration rate of women has increased tremendously since the enactment of the drug policies of the 1980s. The incarceration rate of black women has far surpassed that of their white sisters, and they continue to be overrepresented within the population of incarcerated women at both the state and federal levels, particularly for drug offenses. Nationally, the number of adults, both female and male, who were held in state or federal prisons increased dramatically between 1985 and 1996 and between 1985 and 2006; there was a slight decrease between 1996 and 2006. In 1985 the total number of sentenced adult inmates under state or federal jurisdiction totaled 522,084. Of this number, 12,400 were white females, and 11,800 were black females. By 1996 the total number of state or federal inmates in the U.S. increased to 1,138,984. Of this population, 33,800 were white women, and 33,900 were black women.[11] By 2006 the total number of prisoners in state or federal prison was 1,570,861.[12] Of this number, 112,498 were women[13]; 49,100 were white women, and 28,600 were black women.[14] The rate of adult prisoners per 100,000 adult residents throughout the United States decreased from 27 to 23 for white females and increased from 183 to 188 for black females from 1985 to 1996.[15] By 2006 the rate was up to 48 for white women and down to 148 for black women.[16]

The presence of black females in the criminal justice system is seldom studied. Even when criminologists attempt to place black females at the center of their research regarding the processing of females by the criminal justice system, such studies tend to be piecemeal and incomplete. This problem often derives from the lack of data sources that provide information with regard to the intersection of race and sex throughout the criminal justice process.[17] The result is that the experiences of black females in the criminal justice system, as with other areas of society like employment and income, are often ignored or marginalized. This review places black women at the center of the analysis in order to determine how they have been impacted by the drug policies related to crack cocaine at the federal level. The experiences of all people in the criminal justice system are important—but also different. As feminist criminologists once

---

percent of the adult US population, female and male combined.
11   BJS, 1997.
12   William J. Sabol, Heather Couture and Paige Harrison. "Prisoners in 2006." *Bureau of Justice Statistics Bulletin*. Washington, DC: Department of Justice, 2007,Table 3.
13   Sabol, Couture, Harrison, 2006, Table 3.
14   Sabol, Couture, Harrison, 2006, Table 7.
15   BJS, 1997.
16   Sabol, Couture, Harrison, 2006, Table 9.
17   Mann, 1995.

said, when looking at the experiences of women in the criminal justice system, you cannot simply "add color and stir."[18] Although there may be common attributes and experiences among all women, race and ethnicity provide different lenses through which women see the world and are seen by the world. This is no less true in criminal justice than in other areas of life and society.

This policy review will provide an in-depth analysis of various aspects of the war on drugs on black women. It will include a presentation of background information regarding the growth in the number of people—both female and male of a variety of races—who have been incarcerated in U.S. prisons for drug offenses in the two decades after the implementation of the drug policies. This discussion also includes statistics of how the drug laws are related to the incarceration of people based upon race and gender separately. It continues with a focus on women and drugs, showing the pronounced link between the incarceration of women in general and black women specifically and the evolution of the drug laws. This approach—including how the war on drugs has impacted all people in general, as well as black women specifically—provides context. Black women occupy a unique position in society, as do all groups. Black women's experiences are influenced by their race and their gender. Therefore, to fully understand the impact of these laws on black women, one should begin by uncovering what the impact has been on people of the same or different races and gender.

A thorough discussion of the war on drugs, with a focus on the 100:1 ratio for powdered and crack cocaine (the law that requires a person be convicted of one hundred times more powdered cocaine than crack cocaine to receive the same sentence) will be addressed, providing the reader with an understanding of what the ratios mean in a practical sense. For the purposes of this policy review, the *war on drugs* is defined as: the application of mandatory minimum penalties for drug offenses that involve crack cocaine that are included in the Anti-Drug Abuse Acts of 1986 and 1988.

The enactment of the drug policies of 1986 and 1988 occurred within a social environment that was influenced by political pressures, sensationalism within the media, an absence of research, and a push for law and order. The factors that constructed this environment and their roles in the war on drugs are explained. In the decades to follow, various groups pushed for lessening the perceived harshness of mandatory minimum sentencing on low-level drug offenders. A review of some of these proposals, both adopted and pending, will be provided.

As a former legislator, I can relate to the adage: "You never want to see how laws and sausage are made." Having been in those back rooms where decisions

---

18   Sally Simpson. "Feminist Theory, Crime, and Justice." *Criminology* 27.4 (1989): 605–631.

are made that impact peoples' lives, I know that it is important for citizens to understand just how laws are developed, enacted, and implemented. It is more than simply understanding what we learn in government or political science courses. To truly understand the legislative process, one must be aware of the internal and external forces that shape the process and the policies, and it is my hope that more informed citizens will become part of the legislative and policy-making process. To that end I will discuss two perspectives to provide some understanding of how the policies may have interacted with politics and bureaucracy, resulting in the initial effect of the laws on the incarceration of black women, as well as some of the groups that have applied political pressure for changes to federal crack cocaine policies. The two perspectives that I will discuss are: William Chambliss's conflict theory of law, order, and power[19] and Stuart Scheingold's cultural interpretation of the politicization of crime.[20]

Chapter two will continue with a discussion of terms that are integral to this policy analysis, such as: *disproportionality, overrepresentation,* and *criminal justice systems.* An overview of the presence of black women in the prisons will be presented and discussed.

Chapter three provides background information about the users of crack and the imprisonment of drug offenders, including black women. It also provides a definition of the term *war on drugs.* Historically, women in the United States have been major consumers of both legal and illegal drugs.[21] Information about this relationship, as well as the connection between drugs and the imprisonment of women, is outlined.

Chapter four discusses what is commonly referred to as the war on drugs: its history and content and its intimate relationship with politics and the media. The drug policies, particularly mandatory minimum sentencing for drug offenses, are reviewed comprehensively. The alternative sentencing schemes that have been enacted since 1988 and used in the federal system to attempt to lessen the punitive impact of the drug laws will be reviewed. Because the two forms of cocaine (crack and powdered) are at the nexus of the drug war, discussions about the administration and effects of each form are also included.

Chapters five, six, and seven provide an overview of the specific questions that are pertinent to this investigation, as well as the findings from the analyses of the data. These analyses include investigating the relationships between the imposition of mandatory minimum sentencing in drug cases, the decision to

---

19   William Chambliss and Robert Seidman. *Law, Order, and Power.* (Reading, MA: Addison-Wesley Publishing Co, 1971).

20   Stuart A Scheingold. *The Politics of Law and Order: Street Crime and Public Policy.* (N.Y.: Longman, 1984).

21   Craig Horowitz. February 5, 1996. "The No-Win War," *New York Magazine,* 22–33.

incarcerate, and the length of sentence imposed on female drug offenders in general and black women specifically in 1996 and in 2006, representing ten and twenty years, respectively, after the inception of the war on drugs. I also analyze the use of the alternative sentencing options, that is, safety valves and downward departures. The specific focus of this policy review is to determine to what degree the disproportionately high number of incarcerated black females is related to the mandatory minimum sentencing laws attached to offenses involving relatively low levels of crack cocaine. In other words, how are the laws regarding crack cocaine related to the incarceration of black women? Is crack cocaine a major reason for the number of black women in prison, and if so, is it because the women were involved with large amounts of crack; because they had extensive prior criminal records; and/or because the law requires imprisonment for relatively small amounts of crack cocaine? Furthermore, has the impact changed in the last twenty years, and if so, how?

Chapter eight broaches the question of how the impact on black women could be allowed to continue for so long. This chapter includes a detailed discussion of the politicization of crime and the resultant effect on criminal justice policy. The case is made for using a non-essentialist approach to research that involves gender instead of ignoring the racial, if not ethnic, differences among women.[22] Consequently, the marginalization of black females in the United States becomes a relevant issue that is presented as part of this analysis. Chapter eight also presents a review of prior research regarding the sentencing of black females.

Chapter nine will discuss the findings and the practical impacts on black women, their children, and their communities. This chapter also discusses what has and has not changed at the federal level in the decades since the enactment of the crack cocaine policies, and it includes a discussion of who some of the women are who have been incarcerated for crack cocaine offenses and the obstacles they will face upon their release. Federal initiatives that are being considered at the time of the completion of this book are presented.

Although there is commonality among the experiences of all females in this study, the differences that exist between females of different races, and in many instances, ethnicities, are not treated as nuances. These differences are treated as more than simply "context" or "magnitude."[23] Females in this study were not artificially defined by their race or their gender. Their status as black,

---

22   Adrien K. Wing. "Essentialism and Anti-Essentialism: Ain't I a Woman?" *Critical Race Feminism.* (NY: New York University, 1997); Daly, Kathleen and Lisa Maher. "Crossroads and Intersections: Building from Feminist Critique." *Criminology at the Crossroads.* (NY: Oxford University Press,1998).

23   Harris, 1997, 14.

Hispanic, or white females is treated on a holistic basis. Consequently, the status of being a black female is not divided into separate variables of race and sex, nor are these variables considered to be additive or interactive. Instead, black, white, and Hispanic women are all left whole; race and gender are not artificially extracted as variables but are used as demographic criteria for the selection of the samples.

Black females are at the center of this research. Their experiences are highlighted and become the standard to which the experiences of their Hispanic and white counterparts are compared. The development of the research includes and attempts to explain the specific effects of the war on drugs on black females, thus providing important information about the experiences of black females in the federal prison system. Comparisons within and among samples of black, white, and Hispanic females provide important information about the common and unique experiences of these three groups of women.[24] The current study separates the women into racial groups (black and white females) and one ethnic group (Hispanic females) in order to answer several of the research questions separately for each group.[25] Neither this research nor the underlying theory assumes a position of racial essentialism and is therefore not offered as equally applicable to black males. There are sufficient studies and increasing research findings about black males that provide a basis for comparison between the two groups.

---

24 A purely anti-essentialist approach would require that the data be collected and analyzed on an individual basis. This would allow for the analysis of all or most factors that make each woman unique, even as compared to other females within her racial group. Quantitative research makes such level of evaluation very difficult, and the data analyzed in this study do not readily support such analysis. The data points do, however, provide important information that, along with qualitative research methods, allow for more individualized analyses, and increase knowledge about the impact of public policies such as the war on drugs.

25 In separate volumes, the focus will be placed on the relationship between the war on drugs and each of the other two groups: Hispanic and white females.

—————————CHAPTER TWO—————————
The Imprisonment of Black Women

Stephanie N. – Twenty-Six Years for Crack Conspiracy[26]

Stephanie was twenty-three years old in 1990 when she was convicted of being part of a crack cocaine conspiracy. The mother of four, who was pregnant with her fifth child at the time, had no prior criminal record. Five men were part of the conspiracy, one of whom had been her boyfriend for six weeks. Stephanie knew he was a drug dealer but had no idea that he and two of the other men would say she was guilty of the drug offenses. As a result, she received more time than the three men received combined.

Sentence: twenty-six years for crack conspiracy

Before we investigate the impact of the war on drugs on the imprisonment of black women, it is important to understand what is meant by these terms: *prison systems* and *disproportionality* (or *overrepresentation*).

In the United States, there are fifty state criminal justice and prison systems and one federal system. The states each have laws that are enacted by their state legislatures and governors that determine what behaviors constitute crimes and what the corresponding punishments should be. There is also a federal criminal justice system. The federal criminal laws are enacted by Congress and signed into law by the president. These laws are also applicable in the states under certain circumstances. These circumstances may be determined by: (1) where the crime took place (for example, airport and

---

26   http://November.org/thewall/cases/nod-s/nod-s.html. 11/27/2009.

federal buildings) or (2) the specifics of the law itself (which allow states' attorney generals to decide to notify the federal authorities and transfer a case from state jurisdiction to the federal jurisdiction). In this book, the term *prison system* refers to both the state and federal systems unless otherwise stated. *Disproportionality* and *overrepresentation* both basically mean that a group's presence within the subject area, for instance prison, does not reflect their presence in the general population. For example, black people are approximately 12 percent of the general population within the United States. If they were proportionately represented in the prison populations, they would make up approximately 12 percent of the prison population. If they constitute a significantly higher percentage of the prison population—for example, 36 percent—they are considered to be disproportionately represented because they are over-represented, that is, their numbers are three times higher in the prison population as compared to the general population. In the same way, if a group makes up 70 percent of the general population but only 30 percent of the prison population, they are considered to be disproportionately represented because they are *underrepresented* in the prison population based upon what would be expected due to their numbers in the general population.

A practical application of these concepts is as follows: the presence of black females in the prison system has increased dramatically since the mid 1980s. Although black females constituted only 12.4 percent of the noninstitutionalized population of women in the United States in 1999, they comprised approximately 50 percent of the population of women who were imprisoned.[27] This means that they were disproportionately as well as overrepresented among the incarcerated female population, with numbers more than four times what would be expected based upon their presence in the general population of women in the United States. By understanding the concepts of disproportionality and overrepresentation, we are able to appreciate that a racial group does not have to constitute the majority of a prison population in order to be overrepresented therein.

When did this increased presence of black women within female prison populations begin? History indicates that major growth in the number of imprisoned black women can be traced to the 1980s. Between 1980 and 1992, the number of black women in state and federal prisons increased by 278 percent, while the number of black men increased by 186 percent. During that time, the overall prison population (including white males and females and other demographic groups) grew by 168 percent.[28] In addition to

---

27   Bureau of Justice Statistics. <u>Correctional Populations in the United States, 1996</u>. (Washington, DC: Department of Justice, U.S. Census, 1990).

28   Mark Mauer and Tracey Huling. *Young Black Americans and the Criminal Justice System: Five Years Later*. (Washington, DC: The Sentencing Project, 1995) 19.

having the highest percentage increase in the number of incarcerated persons of any demographic group, black women also saw the greatest increase in the percentage who were under the supervision of the criminal justice system (jail or prison, parole or probation) with a rate of increase of 78 percent between 1989 and 1994.[29] Being under criminal justice supervision, even if one is not incarcerated but on parole or probation, restricts a person's freedom. This increased scrutiny may also increase a person's likelihood of being sent to prison because the person on parole or probation need not commit a new crime in order to be incarcerated. She may also be incarcerated for a technical violation (for example, not reporting to meet with her parole officer on a certain day at a certain time).

Why were so many black women imprisoned during the 1980s and early 1990s? Why were black women so overrepresented within the population of incarcerated females? The drug laws proved to be a significant factor. The single largest category of offenses for which black women were imprisoned was the violation of drug laws. Furthermore, many of the black women convicted of drug offenses were charged with crimes that involved small amounts of crack cocaine. These convictions carried with them mandatory minimum sentences that required the imprisonment of people found guilty of drug offenses that involved relatively low levels of crack cocaine. These mandatory provisions were enacted by the United States Congress as part of the Anti-Drug Abuse Acts of 1986 and 1988 (that is, the war on drugs). These provisions are still law. Publicity about the war on drugs has declined; however, the enforcement of the drug policies that constitute the war on drugs continues.[30]

Other research on sentencing and the processing of black females through the criminal justice system has also found disparity, specifically, differences in sentencing or processing that cannot be explained by legal factors such as prior record or type of offense. Certainly, when disparity of treatment by decision makers such as police officers, judges, and prosecutors exists, it adds to disproportionality. It is also possible, however, that certain laws may require disparity. A point in fact, is the 100:1 ratio that distinguishes offenses for crack cocaine and powdered cocaine. Under the current drug policies, although crack cocaine is a derivative of powdered cocaine, one hundred times more powdered cocaine than crack cocaine is required to trigger mandatory minimum sentences of imprisonment. Furthermore, when powdered cocaine is weighed for the purpose of determining if the statutory threshold has been met, only the pure cocaine substance is counted in the weight. In contrast, when crack cocaine is weighed, the filler, such as sodium

---

29   Mauer and Huling, 1.

30   Katherine Beckett and Theodore Sasson. *The Politics of Injustice*. (California: Pine Forge Press, 2000).

bicarbonate, is included in the total weight that determines if the threshold amount is attained to trigger mandatory minimum sentencing.[31] Thus, the law itself requires disparity in the treatment of women who are convicted of offenses that involve the two forms of cocaine. This disparity was inherent in the drug laws contained in the Anti-Drug Abuse Acts of 1986 and 1988, and this disparity exacerbated the disproportionality of black women in the population of incarcerated females in the 1980s and 1990s. Now that more than twenty years have passed since the enactment of both the 1986 and 1988 Anti- Drug Abuse Acts, an additional question to be addressed is whether the impact of these drug policies on the disproportionate representation of black women within the population of federally incarcerated women continues to exist.

Although the mandatory minimum sentencing laws for crack cocaine were enacted more than two decades ago, they are still a part of the drug policies that are currently implemented.[32] As a former legislator, I know that it is very difficult to convince legislators to repeal or significantly change existing laws, particularly criminal laws. Many of them may agree that the change is needed but are faced with the concern that they may seem "too soft on crime." Such a label, even if unfounded, can be used by opponents to unseat them, particularly when some media prefer to incite the emotions of their readers or viewers rather than provide substantive facts. There are instances, though, when a window of opportunity may appear that allows for change. Although the Anti-Drug Abuse Acts of 1986 and 1988 have not been significantly altered, there have been several adjustments made to the sentencing policies that may have lessened the impact of the drug laws for crack cocaine on the incarceration of black women in federal prisons. It is therefore important to know what the impact of the underlying federal drug polices for crack cocaine are approximately twenty years after their inception, as well as the impact of the other policies that mitigate their punitiveness in certain cases. Ultimately the question is whether these modifications are sufficient. Are they punishing the people (women) who the law was intended to punish for involvement in crack cocaine offenses? Are the black women who have been sent to federal prison for crack cocaine offenses the appropriate targets of these laws? In other words, are they the drug kingpins the laws were ostensibly intended to target, or are they unintended victims caught in the crossfire of the war on drugs?

---

31   United States Sentencing Commission. *Special Report to the Congress: Cocaine and Federal Sentencing Policy.* (Washington, DC: U.S. Government Printing Office, 2007).

32   21 USC 13 Sections 841,844, 846.

CHAPTER THREE
Race, Gender, Drugs, and Imprisonment

Danielle M. – Life in Prison for Cocaine Conspiracy[33]

At age twenty-six, Danielle, the mother of two young children, was sentenced to three life sentences plus twenty years for cocaine-related offenses. She was a first-time, nonviolent offender. Her husband was accused of conspiracy to distribute five kilograms of cocaine. Shortly thereafter, Danielle was arrested and told by the police that they were not after her but rather her husband. She was strongly urged to tell what she knew or never see her children again. Danielle indicates she could not and would not cooperate and that it took more than a year before the government found witnesses to testify against her. The witnesses were people who were accused or convicted of drug-related charges and seeking sentence reductions. Some of them were reportedly serving thirty-year sentences until they testified against Danielle and others, at which time most were moved to halfway houses or freed.

Danielle admits to "completing various tasks at my husband [sic] request including collection [sic] drug money. While I my [sic] actions should not have gone unpunished I feel that my sentence was unfair. If anything, my most serious offense was trying to salvage a failing marriage."[34]

Sentence: life in prison for cocaine conspiracy

---

33   http:/November.org/thewall/cases/metz-d/metz-d.html. 11/27/2009.
34   Homepage of Danielle Metz. http://freedom-for-danielle-metz.com/. 11/27/2009.

A black woman's experiences are influenced by her race (black), gender (female), and the intersection of the two (black female).[35] Both race and gender are social constructs. A *social construct* is defined by society's expectations of a person based upon such things as the person's race (skin color, culture, language, nationality, etc.) or gender (expectations based upon biological sex). Social constructs, including race and gender, are very subjective and value-laden and are determined both by how the person self-identifies as well as how others perceive them to be. Take, for example, a person who has mixed heritage, with one parent being of European descent (white) and the other being of African descent (black). The individual may identify himself as being either black or white or both; others may define the person more by skin color, hair texture, or other factors the perceiver deems relevant. In either case, the determination of the person's race is a subjective decision that is informed by both the personal and the social experiences of the decision maker. An example of this would be President Obama who is most often considered to be black although his mother was white and his father was black. In the same manner, we often observe that the roles a female is expected to fulfill in her family and community are not simply defined by her biological sex (female) but also by the values and customs of her society or community. A woman's gender roles are often greatly influenced by her race, ethnicity, and culture. We therefore begin with a review of how race and gender, as separate constructs, are related to drug use as well as imprisonment for drugs. This will be followed by a focus on black women.

Who Uses Crack: Public Perception versus Facts

When asked about their use of crack in 1991, 52 percent of those who reported they had used crack at least once were white, 38 percent were black, and 10 percent were Hispanic. Approximately ten years later, the percentage of those who reported using crack at least once in their lives had increased for whites (69 percent), decreased for blacks (16 percent), and slightly increased for Hispanics (10.6 percent).[36]

Overall, 0.3 percent of the whites who responded to the survey, 1.5

---

35   I understand that race and gender are social constructs, defined by society's expectations based upon one's color, ethnicity, and/or culture (race) or biological sex (gender). For purposes of this book, I am using the term *black* to refer to people of African descent, including but not limited to African Americans; and *gender* as the biological sex of either female or male.

36   Source: NHSDA in 1991 as reported by United States Sentencing Commission Report, 1995: 32–34; SAMSHA, Office of Applied Studies, National Survey on Drug Use and Health, 2002 and 2003, adapted from Tables 1.42B and 1.43B.

percent of the blacks, and 0.6 percent of the Hispanics reported using crack at least once in 1991.[37] By 2003 the percentages remained quite similar: 0.5 percent for whites, 1.5 percent for blacks, and 0.5 percent for Hispanics.[38] The National Household Survey on Drug Abuse (NHSDA) discovered that 2.8 percent of the whites, 3.9 percent of the blacks, and 3.8 percent of the Hispanics who were surveyed in 1991 reported use of cocaine in any form. In 2003 the results were 2.5 percent for whites, 2.7 percent for blacks, and 3.1 percent for Hispanics.[39] Thus, based upon each group's presence in the general population, the majority of those reporting that they used cocaine were white.[40] Because whites make up a much larger percentage of the general population, based upon these results, it would be expected that the majority of people who are arrested, convicted, and imprisoned for offenses involving crack cocaine, would be white; however, this is not the case.

In 1997 a similar study was conducted that differentiated between crack and powdered cocaine on the basis of demographic groups (that is, whether the person responding was a black female, white female, Hispanic female, black male, etc.). The results indicated that white males and white females reported the greatest use of crack among their respective groups by gender. In other words, more of the white females than the black or Hispanic females who responded said that they had used crack.[41] Even in 2007, the responses were similar: 22.4 percent of the white females, 5.3 percent of the black females, and 3.5 percent of the Hispanic females reported having ever used crack. Among the males who responded in 2007, 44.8 percent of the white males, 13.2 percent of the black males, and 6.8 percent of the Hispanic males reported similar use.[42] Although some people who answer questions about their use of drugs may not be totally honest and one would not expect that the exact percentages are true, the trends—who uses crack cocaine the most or least—provide useful information. Based upon the results, once again, it could be expected that far more white females and males would be arrested and convicted of crack cocaine offenses than their black or Hispanic counterparts. However, the reported use of drugs by blacks, whites, and Hispanics does not reflect the racially disproportionate patterns

---

37 USSC, 1995.34.

38 SAMSHSA, Office of Applied Studies, National Survey on Drug use and Health, 2002 and 2003, Table 1.43B.

39 SAMSHSA, Office of Applied Studies, National Survey on Drug use and Health, 2002 and 2003, Table 1.42B.

40 USSC, 1995.

41 Source: Substance Abuse and Mental Health Services Administration, Office of Applied Studies, adapted from the *1997 National Household Survey on Drug Abuse.*

42 Source: Substance Abuse and Mental Health Services Administration, Office of Applied Studies, adapted from the 2007 National Survey of Drug Use and Health, 2007.

of drug arrests, convictions, or incarceration of black people. Although black people are not the group that reportedly uses crack cocaine the most, they are consistently the group that has been most often arrested, convicted, and incarcerated for drug offenses involving crack cocaine. In 1996, 85.8 percent of the people who were convicted for offenses involving crack cocaine and sentenced in the federal courts were black, 8.7 percent were Hispanic, and 4.8 percent were white.[43] Though blacks constituted the greatest percentage of people convicted in the federal system for drug offenses that involved crack cocaine, this was not consistent with the reported use of drugs by each group.

The percentages changed slightly in 2007, but the trends remained similar to those in 1996: blacks constituted the greatest percentage of people who were convicted and sentenced in the federal systems for drug offenses involving crack cocaine (82.7 percent), which was once again inconsistent with the reported drug use among the three racial/ethnic categories.

Following the federal drug law initiatives of 1986 and 1988, there was an increase in the arrest and imprisonment of black people (male and female) who were deemed users and sellers of crack cocaine. Although black people have consistently constituted approximately 13 percent of the general population, in 1976 they represented 22 percent of the arrests in the United States (both state and federal systems) for violations of drug laws (as compared to 77 percent for whites). By 1990 the percentage of arrests that involved blacks nationwide increased to 41 percent and had decreased to 59 percent for whites; by 2006 a decrease was reported for blacks at 35.1 percent and an increase for whites, up to 63.6 percent.[44] Although the percentages changed each of these years, one can see that blacks were consistently overrepresented within the population of people who were arrested.

As we look at the federal criminal justice system specifically, federal data indicate that 37.5 percent of all defendants who were convicted of drug offenses in federal court in 1993 were black, and 60.5 percent were white. In 2006 the percentages for black offenders decreased to 29.2 percent (more than two times their percentage of the general population) and decreased for white offenders to 25.8 percent; but a new category appeared, Hispanics, at 41.7 percent. Prior to that time, Hispanics were included in the categories of white or black. Therefore the decreases in percentages of black and white offenders are most likely the result of the addition of this third category, Hispanic, which drew its numbers from the other two categories. (For example, black

---

43   Source Adapted from *Sourcebook of Criminal Justice Statistics 1997*, Table 5.38, page 415; U.S. Sentencing Commission, 2007 Datafile, USSCFY07, Table 34.

44   U.S. Department of Justice, FBI, Crime in U.S., 2006, Table 43.

Hispanics would now be counted as Hispanic and not black, thus decreasing the number of black people.)

Conviction is just one part of the criminal justice process. After one is convicted of a crime, the judge decides whether to send the person to prison or to order an alternative sentence, such as probation or supervised release. In 1996, of the black female and male offenders convicted of drug offenses, 94.7 percent were sentenced to incarceration, while only 87.9 percent of the white offenders who were convicted of drug offenses were imprisoned. By 2003 there was a slight increase in imprisonments in both categories, rising to 95.3 percent for black offenders and 91.1 percent for white offenders.[45] The decision to incarcerate could be influenced by several legal factors including: if there was a mandatory minimum sentence required for the crime; the defendant's prior record and role in the offense; and whether the defendant provided assistance to the prosecutor, to name just a few. There are also extralegal factors that are sometimes inappropriately considered by the decision makers. These extralegal factors can include the race or gender of the defendant, the socioeconomic status of the defendant, and how the defendant presents herself in court.

Disparity is also found in the length of sentence received among drug offenders by race. Black offenders (female and male) consistently received longer median sentences than their white counterparts. The median sentence for blacks incarcerated for federal drug offenses in 1993 was 74.0 months (6.16 years), as compared to 54.0 months (4.5 years) for whites; ten years later in 2003, the median sentence for blacks was 84.0 months (7 years) and 46.0 months (3.84 years) for whites. As a point of comparison, the median sentence of 84.0 months (7 years) for blacks imprisoned for *drug* offenses in 2003 was two years longer than the median sentence imposed on whites who were convicted of and imprisoned for *violent* crimes (60 months or 5 years).[46]

In summary, although black people are arrested, convicted, and imprisoned disproportionately for violations involving crack cocaine, reported drug use by blacks, whites, and Hispanics do not support the patterns. Furthermore, neither the public's perception nor the media's representation that most people who use crack are black people who live in the inner cities is supported by the data.

As stated by Mark Mauer and Ryan King, "Despite the fact that two-thirds

---

45   U.S. Dept. of Justice, BJS, Compendium of Federal Justice Statistics, 2003, NCJ 210299 (Washington, DC); Dept. of Justice, 2005, p.76 (Table 5.20.2003).

46   BJS, 2003.77--78.

of regular crack cocaine users are white or Latino, 82 percent of the defendants sentenced in federal court for crack offenses are African American."[47]

Women and Drugs

Women in the United States have a long history of abusing both legal and illegal drugs. At the time of the passage of the Harrison Act in 1914, approximately one million of the ten million people then living in the United States were addicted to drugs. Most of these addicts were housewives who were addicted to opiates that they could legally purchase over the counter as medicinal remedies for any number of ailments.[48] Unfortunately, research on the use of drugs focused on males. Some researchers considered drug abuse a male problem because they believed that sociocultural factors caused some men to abuse narcotics while these same factors protected females from such activity. This position prevailed for nearly fifty years. During the 1970s, the women's movement and the "American drug crisis" of the 1960s caused attention to finally be paid to the use of drugs by females.[49]

Historically, women were prescribed drugs such as sedatives and tranquilizers at a much greater rate than their male counterparts. More middle-class women than men are treated in emergency rooms for overdoses of prescription drugs. This has also become a problem for women of lower economic status who are on Medicaid. Initial studies indicated that, although females used illegal drugs at a much lower rate than males, the use of drugs by females was much higher than had been assumed previously. During the period from 1967 to 1972, studies revealed that the rate of increase in the use of drugs by females was much greater than that of males, including the heroin epidemic of the 1960s.[50]

Researchers have discovered that suburban, middle-class women with drinking problems and their inner-city counterparts who use heroin or crack, undergo similar processes during the onset of drug use.[51] Both groups of women have similar motives for taking drugs and share many of the same experiences that take them from experimentation to addiction. Depression often precedes the use of drugs by women, and drugs of any type may be used to deal with the depression. Some women use drugs as a means of self-medication to cope with the devaluation of women in general and the

---

47   Marc Mauer and Ryan S.King. *A 25-Year Quagmire: The War on Drugs and Its Impact on American Society.* (Washington, DC: The Sentencing Project, 2007), 21.

48   Horowitz, 1993.

49   Horowitz, 1993.

50   James A. Inciardi, Dorothy Lockwood, and Anne E. Pottieger. *Women and Crack-Cocaine.* (NY: Macmillan Publishing, 1993).

51   Inciardi, Lockwood, and Pottieger, 1993.

resultant low self-esteem. Traumas of a personal nature, such as rape, incest, and other forms of sexual abuse, as well as economic pressure, may also lead to drug abuse by women. The combination of being devalued because they are women, minorities, and poor is also posited as an underlying cause for drug abuse by some women. Drug use by any woman, whether she lives in a suburban or urban area, brings with it the psychological, social, and cultural experience of stigmatization that can cause the continued use of drugs. This usage and its inherent problems violate the gender expectations established for women by this society. Women's drug use often leads to social isolation, cultural denigration, and feelings that help to perpetuate the problematic behavior. Also, women have been found to be more likely than men to continue their use of drugs after initial experimentation as a way to cope with situational factors, life events, or general psychological distress.[52]

Poor women who use street-level drugs experience additional stigmatization. They do not have the protective societal buffer enjoyed by women who are insulated from this stigma by family, friends, and economic status. Women who use street-level drugs tend to suffer greater criticism, denigration, and loss of relationships.[53] Women who use these drugs, such as crack cocaine, on the streets are also less protected from becoming prisoners of the war on drugs because of their high visibility.[54] Women have a greater role to play in the distribution of crack cocaine as compared to other drugs. Although the drug market is not "an equal opportunity employer," and women don't tend to benefit financially from the drug market, as do men, they often buy the firearms or rent the residences that are used to support the crack cocaine business enterprise. Because the tactics of the drug initiatives focus upon (a) street-level drugs such as cocaine, crack, and heroin; and (b) street-level offenses such as possession and trafficking, the group of women who participate in these activities will predictably constitute a major portion of the incarcerated population who are sentenced for committing a drug offense.

Drug use among women who are arrested is quite prevalent. Forecasting is a method often utilized to get an idea of the prevalence of drug use among people who are arrested. Forecasting the use of drugs consists of voluntary tests of arrestees' urine, which is analyzed on an anonymous basis. These tests are conducted at the time of arrest, which may be a significant period of time after the commission of the alleged offense. During 1994, screening for the use of drugs was performed on adult females who were booked at

---

52   Inciardi, Lockwood, and Pottieger, 1993.

53   Inciardi, Lockwood, and Pottieger, 1993; Lisa Maher. *Sexed Work*. (Oxford: Clarendon Press, 1997).

54   Horowitz, 1993.

twenty-one sites. Cocaine proved to be the preferred drug among the adult female arrestees. In all but one site, the percentage of female arrestees who tested positive for cocaine exceeded the percentage who tested positive for marijuana. In a number of cases, the rate for the use of cocaine was at least double the rate of marijuana use. Similar results were found in 2000 using Arrestee Drug Abuse Monitoring (ADAM). Similar data were collected from twenty-nine sites, and in twenty-six of these sites, the majority of the women tested positive for at least one of the following drugs: cocaine, opiates, marijuana, methamphetamines, or PSP. In half of the sites, the percentage of women testing positive for one of the five drugs was greater than 63 percent. Once again, cocaine was the drug used most often by the female arrestees (one-third) followed by marijuana (27 percent).[55] It is important to note that, once ingested, the two forms of cocaine (crack and powdered) cannot be distinguished from one another.

Based upon the prevalence of drug use by women in the general population and the prevalence and frequency of drug abuse by female arrestees, it is not surprising that there is a high prevalence in the use/abuse of drugs by female prisoners prior to their incarceration.[56] What is generally not known is that many female prisoners are reportedly involved in drug use more than male prisoners. Women who were imprisoned in state facilities in 1991 reported using more drugs—and also reported using these drugs more frequently—than male prisoners. The use of drugs reported by women who are in prison has increased slightly since the onset of the war on drugs in 1986. In 1986, 50 percent of the women reported using drugs during the month before the offense for which they were incarcerated in state prison; by 1991, this percentage had increased to 54 percent. Among those women, the use of cocaine or crack increased from 23 percent in 1986 to 36 percent in 1991. The use of marijuana decreased (from 30 percent in 1986 to 20 percent in 1991).

Drug use by female inmates is not correlated with violent offenses. In fact, women who were serving prison sentences and who used drugs, irrespective of the frequency and amount of drugs they used, were *less likely* than non-drug users to serve a sentence for a violent offense.[57] Seventeen percent of the female inmates who reported that they had committed their current offense to obtain money for drugs were in prison for a crime that included violence and 43 percent for a crime that involved property. Among the women who committed crimes to obtain money for drugs, 54 percent were incarcerated for robbery, burglary, larceny, or fraud. Only 22 percent of the females who

---

55 National Institute of Justice. 2000 Arrestee, Drug Abuse Monitoring: Annual Report, (Washington, DC: Department of Justice, 2003).

56 BJS, 1994.

57 BJS, 1994.

provided motives other than money for the purchase of drugs for their crime were incarcerated for these economic crimes. In other words, if a female committed an offense, it was very often a nonviolent crime to get money to support her drug habit.

Even with the high prevalence of drug use among female offenders, half of the women in state prisons in 1991 reported never participating in a drug treatment or drug education program.[58]

By 2004 the results were very similar, and 48 percent of the federally incarcerated women reported the use of drugs one month prior to the offense for which they were incarcerated. This was an 11 percent increase in the number who reported such drug use in 1997.[59] The majority of federally incarcerated people who reported having used drugs within one month of their current offense also reported never having participated in drug treatment.[60] Even while imprisoned, only one out of eight women in federal prison receive treatment for substance abuse.[61]

In summary women in federal prison report using drugs more frequently, using harder drugs, and using drugs for reasons different from those of their male counterparts.[62] Few had drug treatment before or during their incarceration.

The Imprisonment of Drug Offenders in the Federal System

Between 1985 and 2006, the number of federal inmates who were incarcerated for drug offenses increased more than ninefold. In 1985 there were 31,364 inmates sentenced in the federal prisons. Thirty-four percent of these inmates (9,482) were serving time for drug offenses. Ten years later, in 1995, the total number of sentenced federal prisoners had almost tripled (88,101), and almost 60 percent (51,737) of the federal prisoners were sentenced for drug offenses. In 1985, drug offenders constituted a minority of the population of federal prisoners (34.3 percent or 9482); by 1995 a majority of the federal prisoners (59.9 percent or 51,737) were drug offenders.[63] Over the same period (1985 to 1995), the percentage of all state prisoners who were convicted of drug

58 BJS, 1994.
59 Christorpher J. Mumola and Jennifer C. Karberg. Drug Use and Dependence, State and Federal Prisoners. (Washington, DC: U.S. Department of Justice 2007) p.3.
60 Mumola and Karberg, 8.
61 Mumola and Karberg, 7.
62 Langdon, Neal P. and Bernadette Pelissier. Gender Differences Among Prisoners in Drug Treatment. Federal Bureau of Prisons, 2001. May 12, 2008. <http://www.bop.gov/news/reserach_reports.jsp#drug>
63 BJS, 1997b, Table 14.

offenses increased by 478 percent (38,900 to 224,900).[64] By 2006 there were a total of 176,268 sentenced federal prisoners. Of that population, 93,751 were sentenced for drug offenses, representing 53 percent of the federally incarcerated population—a decrease in the percentage since 1995, but a major increase in number.[65]

Women, Imprisonment, and the War on Drugs

The war on drugs has greatly affected the number of black, white, and Hispanic women who have been incarcerated during the last two decades. Although drug abuse may have been prevalent among all incarcerated women (black, white, Hispanic) prior to the war on drugs, women were not incarcerated for drug abuse or drug-related offenses at the rate and in the numbers that exist today. The war on drugs was the impetus for the shift in policy that contributed greatly to the increase in the imprisonment of women in the United States. The drug policies contained in the Anti-Drug Abuse Acts of 1986 and 1988 caused more women to be directed into the federal prison system. These policies also subjected more women to greater probability and longer periods of incarceration for low-level drug offenses.

The number of women incarcerated in state prisons for drug offenses increased 433 percent between 1986 and 1991 as compared to an increase of 283 percent for men during the same period.[66] One of every three women imprisoned in prison facilities of the United States in 1991 was incarcerated for a drug offense; in 1979 only one in ten women was incarcerated for drug offenses. Drug offenses represented 55 percent of the national increase in women prisoners from 1986 to 1991.[67] Although there was an increase of 275 percent in the incarceration of females in federal and state prisons between 1980 and 1992, the arrests of females for violent offenses, such as murder, aggravated assault, and robbery, only increased by 1.3 percent (from 10.0 to 11.3 percent).

---

64   BJS, 1997b:10.
65   BJS, Prisoners in 1996 (Tables 10 and 14) and BJS Prisoners in 2006 (Table 12).
66   Barbara Bloom, Cheoleon Lee, and Barbara Owen. *Offense Patterns Among Women Prisoners: A Preliminary Analysis*. Paper presented at the American Society of Criminology Annual Meeting, (Boston, MA, November 1995).
67   BJS, 1994.

Table 3.1: Offenses of Female Inmates (%) in Federal Institutions

Offense type	1981	1991	2006
Violent	7.1	2.0	4.6
Drug	26.0	63.9	61.7
Property	28.2	6.3	15.8

Source: 1981 and 1991: Adapted from table provided by Kline, *Female Offenders: Meeting Needs of a Neglected Population*, 34; 2006, BJS' Federal Justice Statistics Program Website (*http://fjsrc.urban.org*).[68]

In 1981, 7.1 percent of the females who were in federal prisons were incarcerated for violent offenses, 28.2 percent for property offenses, and 26.0 percent for drug offenses. By 1991 the percentages had shifted to 2.0 percent for violent offenses, 6.3 percent for property offenses, and 63.9 percent for drug offenses (Table 3.1).[69] Thus, although there were decreases in the percentage of incarcerated women who were convicted of robbery and violent offenses, the percentage of women who were incarcerated in the federal system for drug offenses more than doubled during this period of the war on drugs. Between 1990 and 1996, there was an increase of 2,057 women who were sentenced and imprisoned under federal jurisdiction. Eighty-four percent of the increase for women was related to drugs, as compared to 71 percent for men.[70] Thus, the female prison population experienced a greater percentage increase than their male counterparts.

The percentages of females incarcerated in federal facilities for violent offenses and property crimes increased between 1991 and 2006; the percentage of women incarcerated for drug offenses remained almost two and a half times higher in 2006 than in 1981. Additionally, drug offenses remained by far the most dominant category of offense for which women were incarcerated in the federal system at about 62 percent in 2006, about 2 percent less than 1991, but more than double the figure for 1981—26 percent.[71] Without a doubt, drug laws and violations have greatly increased the female prison population.

Drug offenses, as the most serious offense for which inmates in the state prison systems were sentenced, also changed significantly between 1985 and 1995.

---

68   *Source* 1981 and 1991; 2006 – BJS' Federal Justice Statistics Program Website (http://fjsrc.urban.org) Data for 2006 – Extract from BOP's Online Sentry System, FY2006 (as standardized by FJSRC).

69   Stephanie R. Bush-Baskette. "The War on Drugs as a War against Black Women." <u>Crime Control and Women</u>. (Thousand Oaks, CA: Sage, 1998).

70   BJS, 1999:3.

71   BJS' Federal Justice Statistics Program website (http://fjsrc.urban.org).

In 1985, 35.1 percent of new commitments of females (women sent to prison in this particular year) to the state system were convicted of violent offenses, 42.1 percent for property offenses, and 13.2 percent for drug offenses. By 1995 the percentages had decreased to 29.5 percent for violent offenses and 28.9 percent for property offenses, and increased to 30.9 percent for drug offenses.[72] The increase in commitments for drug offenses more than doubled in the state system during this ten-year period. This percentage of females incarcerated in state prison in 2003 was up slightly for violent offenses (33 percent) and relatively the same for drug offenses (31.5 percent) and property offenses (28.7 percent) as in 1991. The percentage of drug offenses among women incarcerated in state prisons in 2003 was still more than twice that of 1982.[73]

In comparison, when we look at all of the women who were serving time in prison in 2003, an analysis of the primary offenses for which women who were serving time after sentencing under state jurisdictions in 2003 indicates that nationally, 33.0 percent were sentenced for violent offenses, 28.7 percent for drug offenses, and 31.5 percent for property offenses.[74] This finding is supported by other studies of individual states, as is the growth of this proportion among women incarcerated at the state level.

Almost twice the percentage of women sent to federal prisons, as compared to state prisons, in the 1990s and 2000s were convicted of drug offenses (Tables 2.1 and 2.2). It appears that the federal Anti-Drug Abuse Acts of 1986 and 1988 were even more punitive than most of the states' drug laws. Not only did the percentage of female federal prisoners who were incarcerated for drug offenses increase over the years,[75] there was also a concomitant increase in the length of their sentences (Table 3.2).

---

72   BJS, 1997.

73   Bureau of Justice Statistics, *Correctional Populations in the United States 1995,* (Washington, DC: US Dept. of Justice, 1997); 2003: Bureau of Justice Statistics, "Prisoners in 2004," Washington, DC: Department of Justice.

74   Paige M. Harrison and Allen J. Beck. "Prisoners in 2004." *Bureau of Justice Statistics Bulletin.* (Washington, DC: Department of Justice, 2005).

75   Bureau of Justice Statistics, *Correctional Populations in the United States 1995,* (Washington, DC: US Dept. of Justice, 1997); 2003: Bureau of Justice Statistics, "Prisoners in 2004," Washington, DC: Department of Justice.

Table 3.2: Change in Average Sentence Length in Months for Federal Offenders, 1982 ,1991, and 2002

Type of Offense	1982	1991	Change between 1982 and 1991	2002	Change between 1991 and 2002
Violent	133.3	90.7	-42.6	88.6	-2.1
Drug	54.6	85.7	31.1	76.0	-9.7

Source: U.S. Dept. of Justice, *Federal Criminal Case Processing*, 1982–1993, (Washington, DC: GPO, 1996); *Federal Criminal Case Processing*, 2002, table 6 p. 12.

In 1982 the average sentence length for drug offenders was 54.6 months, and for violent offenders it was 133.3 months. By 1991 the average sentence length for drug offenders had increased to 85.7 months, and for violent offenders it had declined to 90.7 months. Therefore, the average length of sentences for drug offenders increased by 31.1 months, and for violent offenses the mean sentence length decreased by 42.6 months. Some ten years later, in 2002, the average sentence for both violent and drug offenses had decreased to 2.1 months and 9.7 months, respectively. Between 1982 and 2002, there was a decrease of 44.7 months in the mean sentence for violent offenders and an increase of 21.4 months for drug offenders (Table 3.2). Therefore on the average, violent offenders in the federal system experienced a decrease in their sentence lengths while drug offenders faced significantly longer sentences.

The federal government was not alone in its attack on drug offenders. Most states enacted legislation that either mirrored or was similar to the federal laws. One of the states that enacted stringent anti-drug laws was New York. New York began its initiatives against drugs with the enactment of the "Rockefeller Drug Laws" in 1973. These laws required several mandatory sentences of imprisonment for drug offenses and limited plea-bargaining. Major components of the Rockefeller Laws were repealed in 1976 after they were found to have minimal if any effect on the use of drugs or crime in New York.[76] The Rockefeller Laws still required that a person convicted of possessing four ounces, or attempting to sell two ounces of cocaine or heroin, spend a mandatory fifteen years to life in prison.[77] These laws appear to have had an impact on the increase in the prison population in New York. In 1981, 10 percent of the prison population were nonviolent drug offenders, and 60

---

76   Michael Tonry. *Malign Neglect*. (NY: Oxford University Press, 1995).
77   Horowitz, 1996.

percent were violent offenders. In 1994, violent offenders constituted only 33 percent of the incarcerated prison population in New York, and nonviolent drug offenders constituted 45 percent.[78] The Drug Law Reform Act (DLRA) became effective on January 13, 2005, in New York State. The DLRA replaced the indeterminate sentencing provisions of the Rockefeller Drug Laws with determinate sentences and reduced mandatory minimum prison sentences for nonviolent felony drug offenders.[79] The DLRA also reduced the minimum penalty for conviction on the most serious drug charge in New York from fifteen years to life down to eight years in prison for an offender with no prior felonies. People who were serving life sentences were permitted to apply for re-sentencing. In addition, the weight thresholds for the two most serious possession offenses were doubled.[80]

It is clearly evident that the growth in the prison population, particularly at the federal level, was highly correlated to the increase in the number of people who were incarcerated for drug offenses after the enactment of the Anti-Drug Abuse Acts of 1986 and 1988. We also see that the rate of incarceration for black women soared. Black women were eight times more likely than white women to be incarcerated in 2006. So what is the relationship between the incarceration of black women and the enactment and implementation of the Anti-Drug Abuse Acts of 1986 and 1988?

Defining the War on Drugs

The term *war on drugs* is a phrase often used but not defined. In this review the terms *cocaine* and *powdered cocaine* refer to the powdered form of cocaine (cocaine hydrochloride), which is most often inhaled. The terms *crack* and *crack cocaine* refer to the crystallized base form of cocaine, which is generally smoked.

In 1986 the federal government enacted the Anti-Drug Abuse Act. This law would have far reaching impacts on many groups and communities. Unlike drug policies promulgated previously by the federal government, these initiatives focused on the punishment (instead of treatment) of street-level drug offenders who were involved with crack cocaine. The Act of 1986 also established most of the mandatory minimum sentencing penalties for drug trafficking and importation for a number of drugs, including penalties based upon the amount of drugs involved.[81] Table 3.3 below indicates the

---

78   Horowitz, 1996.

79   Indeterminate sentences are terms of imprisonment stated as a range of time. Determinate sentences are finite, definite sentences that may be reduced for good behavior on the part of the prisoner.

80   2004 N.Y. Laws Ch. 738.

81   Beckett and Sasson, 1998, 38.

mandatory minimum sentences for first-time drug offenders as established in the Anti-Drug Abuse Acts of 1986 and 1988.

Table 3.3: Federal Mandatory Minimum Sentences for First-Time Drug Offenders

Drug	5 Years	10 Years
LSD	1 gram	10 grams
Marijuana	100 plants or 100 kilos	1000 plants or 1000 kilos
Crack Cocaine	5 grams	50 grams
Powder Cocaine	500 grams	5 kilos (5,000 grams)
Heroin	100 grams	1 kilo
Methamphetamines	10 grams	100 grams

Sources: 21 USC 13 (I) (D) Sec 841 and adapted from http://www.hr95.org/ Cruel.html#mms.

As shown above, this legislation also mandated disparate treatment for crack cocaine and powdered cocaine by establishing a 100:1 ratio for crack as compared to powdered cocaine. Persons who are convicted of trafficking or dealing five grams or more of crack cocaine receive a mandatory minimum sentence of five years. Conversely, a person must possess at least five hundred grams of powdered cocaine to receive the mandatory minimum sentence of five years. Furthermore, a person who is convicted of trafficking or dealing fifty grams or more of crack cocaine will receive a mandatory minimum sentence of ten years in prison. In comparison, a person has to be convicted of selling five thousand grams of powdered cocaine to receive the same penalty. [82]

The focus on crack cocaine continued with the implementation of the Anti-Drug Abuse Act of 1988. This Act requires mandatory imprisonment for the simple possession of crack cocaine, thereby making this the only substance for which first-time simple possession constitutes a felony.[83] Under the Act, if a person is found guilty of the simple possession of: (a) more than five grams of crack cocaine, and she is a first time offender; (b) greater than three grams of crack cocaine, and she has one prior conviction for the simple possession of crack cocaine, and is convicted of possession; or (c) greater than one gram of crack cocaine in the instant conviction, and she has two or

---

82 USSC, 1995; 21 USC 13 (I) (D) Sec 841.
83 The possession of powdered cocaine, the substance from which crack is derived, is a misdemeanor, and the maximum sentence for simple possession is one year.

more prior convictions for the possession of crack cocaine, she must receive a mandatory minimum sentence of five years.[84] The Act of 1988 also mandates that persons who *attempt or conspire* to commit a drug offense must receive the same penalties as if they actually committed the substantive offense.[85] To date, the initiatives of the 1986 and 1988 Acts have not been modified significantly. However, there have been several attempts to mitigate what has been perceived by many, as the unintended and negative impacts of the laws on arguably unintended targets: nonviolent, low-level drug offenders. Many of these adjustments and their impacts will be discussed and analyzed later in this volume.

One of the major controversies surrounding the mandatory minimum sentencing scheme is the 100:1 ratio for offenses that involve crack cocaine as compared to powdered cocaine. To understand the issue of proportionality in the application of the 100:1 ratio, one should be aware of the street value of the drugs. Drug prices fluctuate. In the 1980s, the price of crack and powdered cocaine both dropped, but in the 1990s, the prices remained constant or increased. In the 1990s, crack was sold at the retail level in quantities that cost five, ten, or twenty dollars for a single dose. A dose ranges from 0.1 to 0.5 grams. Five grams, which triggers a mandatory sentence of five years, equals ten to fifty doses and costs $225 to $750.[86] Thus, depending on the price, a gram of crack may have cost from $45 to $150, one ounce from $400 to $2,800, and one kilogram from $14,000 to $40,000. In comparison, powdered cocaine is sold in five and ten dose units or grams and costs $65 to $100 per gram. Therefore, the five-hundred-gram amount that triggers the mandatory minimum sentence of five years for powdered cocaine represents 2,500 to 5,000 doses, which in the 1990s cost from $32,500 to $50,000 in the 1990s.[87] Further, even at top value, a retail seller of crack can receive five years for selling $750 worth of crack, but a seller of powdered cocaine must sell $50,000 worth of the substance to receive the same sentence. This disparity in the street value and amounts of crack cocaine that trigger the mandatory minimum sentences has led some to argue that the threshold amounts established for crack fall well below what should be classified as a major or serious dealer or trafficker and that these levels actually reflect users and low-level dealers.[88] If this is true, the intent of Congress to: (a) punish major or serious traffickers and (b) to maintain consistency in establishing

---

84   21 USC 13 (I) (D) Sec. 844.
85   21 USC 13 (I) (D) 846.
86   USSC, 1995: 84–6.
87   USSC, 1995: 86-91; USSC, 2007:63, 93.
88   USSC, 1995 and 1997.

the amount of drugs that trigger mandatory minimum sentences has not been met.

For the purposes of this policy review, the *war on drugs* is defined as the application of mandatory minimum penalties for drug offenses that involve crack cocaine that are included in the Anti-Drug Abuse Acts of 1986 and 1988.

There is little focused research on the impact of the war on drugs on black females. Existing research, although sparse in quantity, indicates that the increase in the number of black women who are sentenced to prison and other forms of criminal justice supervision is probably related to mandatory minimum sentencing schemes contained in the Anti-Drug Abuse Acts of 1986 and 1988. These studies, however, have not determined if these drug policies have a statistically significant effect on the sentencing of black women, and if so, if the drug policies impact sentencing differentially among females. That is the goal of this policy analysis.

─────CHAPTER FOUR─────
The Political Evolution of the War on Drugs

Cynthia C. – Thirty Years for Crack Cocaine Conspiracy[89]

In early 1991, Cynthia was on her way to becoming a member of the law enforcement community. Like most of her friends, Cynthia had grown up poor in her small, rural hometown in Florida. Although most of her peers did not complete high school, Cynthia completed a curriculum at an academy and received a certificate of completion. She did this against all odds. She had never been in any trouble. Then she met a new boyfriend. He had cash, and he shared it with her. He never told her he was a crack dealer. Cynthia fell in love with her boyfriend and chose him over her goal of being in law enforcement. She participated in the delivery of drugs, wired money as he asked her to do, and was rewarded by him for following his directions. Cynthia was not at ease with all of this, but before she decided to step away, she was arrested. In March of 1991, she and her boyfriend were arrested after he sold $5,700 worth of crack to undercover agents. Cynthia was in the automobile when this happened and was therefore charged with the sale and the possession. Because she had been a part of his deals a few times prior, she was considered as guilty as him. When all was said and done, Cynthia and her boyfriend were charged with possessing five kilos of crack, and she received the same amount of prison time as he did. The only difference was that she had no control over the business and followed the orders of her boyfriend.

Cynthia's attorney sent a letter to President Clinton asking that he give Cynthia a prison pardon in 2000. The public defender indicated that this had been her first federal trial and that, since the guidelines

---

89   http:/November.org/thewall/cases/clark-c/clark-c.html. 11/27/2009.

were new, not all lawyers knew how harsh the application of Pinkerton liability could be.[90]

Sentence: thirty years for crack cocaine conspiracy

The Enactment of the ADA of 1986 and 1988

To understand how the war on drugs has impacted black women, one must have an understanding of the war on drugs itself. This knowledge should include the history of the onset of the current war on drugs in the United States, including when it began and the roles that the media and politics assumed in the development of the federal policies that constitute the war. Because of the significant difference in the treatment of offenses that involve crack cocaine and powdered cocaine, a discussion about the origins of cocaine, as well as the similarities and differences between powdered and crack cocaine is included. Furthermore, the imprisonment of black people in general and black women specifically for drug offenses that involve crack cocaine is disproportionate to their presence in the general population, a disparity that is not explained by their use of crack cocaine. Based upon both of these indices, it would be expected that the greatest percentage of people arrested and imprisoned for crack cocaine offenses would be white. Relevant data and discussion are presented that help explain these discrepancies between expectations and reality. Additionally, with the shift in drug policy from the treatment of persons with problems of drug abuse to punishment, it is important to remember the relationship between women and drugs.[91]

The War on Drugs

The United States has a history of enacting anti-drug laws at both the local (city and state) and national (federal) levels of government. The first such law was passed as an ordinance in 1875 by the city of San Francisco. This local legislation outlawed the smoking of opium in opium dens. The federal government began to control the use of cocaine in the early 1900s and the use of marijuana in 1937. The Harrison Act of 1914 was the primary legislative vehicle implemented by the federal government to regulate narcotics in

---

90   In *Pinkerton v. United States*, 328 U.S. 640 (1946), derived the "*Pinkerton* doctrine" under which a party to a conspiracy is responsible for any criminal act committed by an associate if it: a) falls within the scope of the conspiracy or (b) is a foreseeable consequence of the unlawful agreement.

91   Chapter three provides historical and contemporary information about women and their consumption of drugs, including some of the causes and social consequences experienced by women who use drugs.

the United States.[92] The popular term *war on drugs* is seldom defined, but Rasmussen and Benson suggest that there are at least two methods by which to determine when a war on drugs begins. The first involves identifying key legislation or presidential announcements. The second employs the direct measurement of changes in the allocation of criminal justice resources to the enforcement of drug laws.[93]

If one uses presidential announcements or legislative initiatives as indices for the beginning of the war on drugs, there are four benchmark periods: 1972, 1982, 1986, and 1988. President Richard M. Nixon declared the initial war on drugs in 1972.[94] In February 1982, President Ronald Reagan also declared a war on drugs. The goals of these wars were to reduce drug use by individuals, stop the flow of drugs into the United States, and reduce drug-related crimes.[95] The declarations were ignored until 1985.[96] In 1986 and 1988, the Anti-Drug Abuse Acts were enacted into law at the federal level. These acts changed the focus from major drug dealers and treatment, to users and street-level dealers, particularly of crack cocaine.

If one uses the allocation of resources as an indicator of the onset of the post-World War II drug wars, it is apparent that 1986 marked a beginning. In 1986, expenditures from federal, state, and local entities for the war on drugs totaled five billion dollars.[97] In 1991 the national drug policy initiatives cost more than ten billion dollars a year. Prior to resigning as the head of the federal government's war on drugs, William Bennett recommended that the budget for the initiatives be doubled in the 1990–1991 fiscal year. He urged the states to further increase their funding for the drug initiatives by ten billion dollars and to increase the number of prison cells intended to confine drug offenders by 85 percent.[98]

In 1995 the federal government spent $13.2 billion on the drug war. Two-thirds of this money was used for law enforcement. This amount does not include the cost of incarcerating convicted drug offenders. If all of the money spent for the direct costs of the war on drugs is accounted for, the total expenditure was approximately $100 billion annually.[99] By 2000 the

92   Eric Jensen and Jurg Gerber. "The Social Construction of Drug Problems: An Historical Overview." *The New War on Drugs: Symbolic Politics and Criminal Justice Policy.* Ed. Eric L. Jensen and Jurg Gerber. (Cincinnati, OH: ACJS/Anderson, 1998) 1–23.

93   David W. Rasmussen and Bruce L. Benson. *The Economic Anatomy of a Drug War.* (Lanham, MD: Rowman and Littlefield Publishers, 1994), 6.

94   Craig Horowitz. "The No-Win War." *New York Magazine.* 5 February 1996: 22–33.

95   Horowitz, 1996.

96   Belenko, 1993, 23.

97   Horowitz, 1996.

98   National Council on Crime and Delinquency. National Drug Statement. (Hackensack, NJ: NCCD, 1991).

99   Horowitz, 1996.

$13.2 billion spent in 1995 had increased to more than $18 billion.[100] Federal statistics provide substantiation of the federal government's increased and harsher response to drug offenders between 1982 and 1991.[101] In 1982, 81.3 percent of individuals who were charged with a drug offense in the federal system were *prosecuted*. In 1988 the percentage had decreased by 4.8 percent to 76.5 percent; however, there was an increase of 52.17 percent in the number of persons *convicted* for drug offenses for those two years (6,979 in 1982, as compared to 13,376 in 1988). Furthermore, in 1982, 5,138 of the persons who were convicted of drug offenses were *incarcerated*. In 1988 the number rose to 10,599, an increase of 48.48 percent.[102] In other words, although there was a decline in the number of persons who were prosecuted for drug offenses in the federal system, there was a significant increase in the percentage of those charged who were convicted and incarcerated for drug offenses. Furthermore, as would be expected given the mandatory minimum sentencing penalties included in the drug laws of 1986 and 1988, the federal drug offenders with minor and no past criminal records, received much longer sentences than similarly situated offenders had received prior to the Anti-Drug Abuse Act of 1986.[103]

What transpired between the declaration of a war on drugs by former President Reagan in 1982 and the legislative initiatives of 1986 sheds light on why only certain kinds of drugs and drug users are targeted by the criminal justice system.

The Role of the Media and Politics in the War on Drugs

The intense media attention that preceded and coincided with national elections sparked development of the drug policies contained within the Acts of 1986 and 1988. Beginning in 1984 and continuing into 1985, the media began reporting about "rock" cocaine in Los Angeles.[104] In 1985 there was a newspaper account of cocaine abuse in New York.[105] These reports were rather obscure, and the public was not overly concerned. However, in 1986,

---

100   National Drug Control Strategy, FY 2001 Budget Summary, p.2, Office of the National Drug Control Policy, 2000.

101   Correctional Populations in the United States, 1993. Bureau of Justice Statistics, 1995; Federal Criminal Case Processing, 2002. Bureau of Justice Statistics, January 2005.

102   BJS, 1995.

103   Tracy Huling. "Prisoners of War: Woman Drug Couriers in the United States." *Drug Couriers: A New Perspective*. Ed. Martin D. Schwartz and Dragan Milovanovic. London: Quartet Books Unlimited, 1996) 58.

104   Belenko, 1993; Beckett and Sasson, 2000; Craig Reinarman and Henry Levine. "The Crack Attack: Politics and the Media in the Crack Scare." *Crack in America*. Ed. Craig Reinarman and Henry Levine (Berkeley: University Press, 1997).

105   Belenko, 1993.

Len Bias and Don Rogers, two well-known athletes, allegedly died from their use of crack cocaine. At that point, the media focused its attention on crack as the issue of the year. All forms of media—newspapers, magazines, and television—began to cover crack cocaine with unprecedented allocations of time.[106] It was determined later that these athletes had not died from their use of crack, but rather from powdered cocaine. However, this factual information received minimal attention from the media, and the media and policy makers' attack on crack cocaine continued, coinciding with an election year. By the elections of November 1986, at least one thousand newspaper stories concerning crack cocaine had appeared in the national print media alone.[107] The major television networks aired documentary-style programs that defined crack cocaine as a national epidemic.[108] Crack cocaine became an ideal campaign issue for politicians.

On October 27, 1986, days before the national elections, the Anti-Drug Abuse Act (ADA) of 1986 was enacted by Congress. This legislation delineated the parameters of the current war on drugs. The emphasis of the ADA of 1986 was on punishment and social control and incorporated such penalties as increased prison sentences for the sale and possession of drugs, elimination of probation or parole for certain drug offenders, increased fines, and the forfeiture of assets. Most of the funds made available as a result of the Act were directed toward law enforcement, expanded prison facilities, interdiction, and efforts to reduce the supply of drugs. The war was contrived as being necessary for the survival of America.[109] Congress expedited the enactment of the Anti-Drug Abuse Act of 1986. There were no committee hearings and little in the congressional record to explain how the 100:1 ratio (of powdered cocaine to crack cocaine) was developed. The record indicates that other ratios were considered such as 50:1 in HR 5484 and 20:1 in S2849, sponsored by Senate Majority Leader Robert Dole on behalf of the administration.[110] Several reasons for the ratios appear in the record. They include:

1. Congress viewed the drug problem as a national "epidemic" in 1986 and considered crack to be the leading drug.

2. Congress deliberately differentiated crack from cocaine.

3. Congress decided that crack was more dangerous than powdered cocaine and decided to treat it differently.

---

106 Belenko, 1993.
107 Craig Reinarman and Henry Levine. "Crack in Context: Politics and Media in the Making of a Drug Scare." <u>Contemporary Drug Problems</u> 16.94 (1989): 535–577.
108 Belenko, 1993.
109 Belenko, 1993, 15.
110 USSC, 1995, 117.

4. Congress wanted to be consistent with other mandatory minimum sentencing provisions by punishing *major* traffickers with a ten-year mandatory minimum prison sentence and *serious* traffickers with a mandatory minimum sentence of five years.[111]

The concepts of *major* and *serious* traffickers are important. Congress defined the terms and outlined their intentions in congressional legislation. Basically, major traffickers were considered "the manufacturers or heads of organizations who are responsible for creating and delivering very large quantities." Serious traffickers were defined as "the managers of the retail level traffic, the person who is filling the bags of heroin, packaging crack cocaine into vials … and doing so in substantial street quantities."[112] In order to select the appropriate level for each drug contained in the legislation of 1986, the subcommittee ordered staff to consult with DEA agents and prosecutors to determine the distribution patterns for various drugs, as well as to determine the amounts that would indicate a person was working at a high level within the market. The subcommittee established the threshold amounts for crack and powdered cocaine without the benefit of hearings.

In 1987, after the national elections and passage of the Anti-Drug Abuse Act of 1986, the media focused its attention on issues other than crack and drug abuse. The public's attention and concern with drugs also declined. The New York Times/CBS polls in 1987 found that only 3 to 5 percent of the public expressed the opinion that drugs were the most pressing social problem.[113] However, during the next presidential election year, drugs—particularly crack cocaine—again became the target of politicians.

In 1988 the media portrayed black and Latina females who used crack cocaine as irresponsible drug addicts who gave birth indiscriminately to children born addicted to crack (otherwise known as "crack babies"). As explained by Drew Humphries:[114]

The American public was introduced to crack mothers by NBC in the 1988 report that featured Tracy Watson, Erocelia Fandino, and Stephanie (October 24 and 25). A pregnant Tracy Watson smoked crack on national television; Erocelia Fandino was shown recovering after giving birth to her premature, cocaine-exposed baby; a street addict named Stephanie, headed for a crack house, told of leaving her baby in the hospital because she had no housing or money. All

---

111 USSC, 1995, 118.
112 H.R. Rep. No. 845, 99th Congress, 2d Session. Pt. 1, at 16-17 (1986).
113 Reinarman and Levine, 1989 and 1997; Beckett and Sasson, 2000.
114 Humphries, 1999, 30–31.

three were active drug users, although they were filmed at home, in the hospital, and on the street.

They were also women of color—black women represented 55 percent of the women shown as drug users on television from 1988 to 1990—and Tracy, Erocelia, and Stephanie belonged to the inner city—a turbulent, drug-infested world set apart from the circumstances of middle-class news audiences. NBC reported that middle-class Americans had stopped using crack (January 13, 1988). The middle class, according to a recovering crack addict, had "too much to lose not to give up drugs" (NBC, May 16 and 17, 1988). On the other hand, drugs were "a way of life in the city," noted another NBC report (May 16 and 17, 1988). That the inner city had crack addicts, added David Musto of Yale University, was understandable. There were no jobs, the schools were inferior, and the future bleak.

Thus, the media portrayed black women who used crack cocaine as "Others"—people unlike the television viewers in morals and lifestyle. As such, these black women became easy targets of the war on drugs. Another Congressional election was about to occur. These representations of black women by the media within an accepting political environment provided congressional candidates with a convenient set of issues on which to run.[115]

Congress passed a subsequent Anti-Drug Abuse Act on October 22, 1988, approximately one and a half weeks before the election. As compared to the 1986 Act, the 1988 Act included more funding for treatment and prevention, and it established the Office of Substance Abuse Prevention as a cabinet-level post. However, most of the funding continued to be directed toward law enforcement and punishment, and enhanced penalties for certain crack cocaine offenses were enacted. The Act amended 21 U.S.C. §844 to make crack the only drug and form of cocaine with a mandatory penalty for the first offense of simple possession. As a result, a person who possesses more than five grams of a mixture or substance that contains cocaine base is to be punished with imprisonment for at least five years. If a person has a prior conviction for possession of crack and is found guilty of having more than three grams of crack, she receives a mandatory minimum of five years in prison. Furthermore, if a person has two or more prior convictions and is found guilty of possessing more than one gram of crack, he also receives a mandatory minimum of five years. This type of penalty is not applied to other drugs. The first conviction for possession of any quantity of any other drug, such as heroin or powdered cocaine, can only result in a maximum penalty

---

115   Reinarman and Levine, 1989, 1997; Craig Reinarman. "The Crack Attack: Politics and Media in America's Latest Drug Scare." *Images of Issues.* Ed. Joel Best. (New York, NY: Aldine De Gruyter, 1990); Beckett and Sasson, 2000.

of one year. In contrast, an offender found guilty of possessing powdered cocaine can only be subjected to a mandatory minimum sentence of five years if the amount equals or exceeds five hundred grams. In 1995 the United States Sentencing Commission recommended to Congress and President Bill Clinton that the disparate treatment between crack and powdered cocaine be abolished because there was no valid reason for the difference in penalty and it was having a negative impact on black people. Neither Congress nor President Clinton supported the recommendation.[116] The Act also provided for civil penalties for the possession and use of crack.[117] The Anti-Drug Abuse bill of 1988 did not include these penalties until it was amended on the floor with little debate.[118] The Department of Justice opposed the amendment.

By 1990 the media representation of crack had stabilized. Most news accounts focused on the health effects of crack and treatment possibilities for the drug's users.[119] Consequently, the National Drug Control Strategy of 1991 did not focus on crack and cocaine as vigorously as did the 1988 legislation. However, the initiatives of the two prior Acts were not significantly modified.

The Anti-Drug Abuse Acts of 1986 and 1988 continue to dictate the fate of drug offenders. They were developed as political responses to heightened public concern about cocaine and crack that resulted from mass media representations.[120] Although attention has been somewhat diverted from crack, cocaine, and drug abuse in general, these policies continue in full force.[121] Since the 1980s there have been several attempts, particularly by the United States Sentencing Commission as well as other organizations, to change the 100:1 ratio for powder cocaine and crack cocaine. These attempts have not been successful in amending the Anti-Drug Abuse Law. There has, however, been some leeway provided through downward departures to increase the discretion of judges in sentencing. These changes as well as other proposed changes to the law will be discussed later in this book.

Mandatory Minimum Sentencing for Drug Offenses

Mandatory minimum sentencing requires that a judge render sentences that are no less than that which is prescribed in the applicable statute. The use of mandatory sentencing schemes began in the United States in 1790 for

---

116 US Sentencing Commission, *Special Report to Congress: Cocaine and Federal Sentencing Policy* (Washington, DC: U.S. Government Printing Office, 1995).

117 Belenko, 1993.

118 USSC, 1995, 124.

119 Belenko, 1993.

120 Reinarman and Levine, 1989 and 1997; Beckett and Sasson, 2000.

121 21 U.S.C 13 Sections 841, 844, 846.

capital offenses.[122] They were used extensively in the Narcotics Control Act of 1956 where they were applied to a great number of drug offenses related to importation and distribution activities. The mandatory minimum sentencing schemes contained in the Narcotics Control Act provided mandatory ranges from which a judge could choose a sentence.[123] The purpose for the mandatory provisions, as set forth by the Senate Judiciary Committee, was to establish the penalties that would be meted out for specific offenses for the purpose of reducing violations of drug laws.[124] During the years subsequent to the Narcotics Control Act of 1956, Congress determined that mandatory minimum sentences were not reducing the number of drug law violations. In response, they enacted the Comprehensive Drug Abuse and Control Act of 1970 and repealed most of the mandatory penalties for the violation of drug laws, except for those related to continuing criminal enterprise.[125] Congress determined that mandatory minimum sentencing: (a) was an obstacle to the rehabilitation of offenders; (b) inappropriately infringed upon judicial discretion; and (c) did not assist in deterrence because prosecutors felt the penalties were too severe and avoided the charges that would invoke the penalties.[126]

In 1984, Congress also reenacted a number of mandatory minimum sentencing schemes that focused on violations of the drug laws. They included: (a) mandatory minimums for drug offenses committed near schools;[127] (b) mandatory minimums or enhancements of sentences for the use of or carrying of a firearm during the commission of certain violent offenses;[128] and (c) mandatory minimum sentences for all serious felonies and also a mandatory minimum sentence of one year probation for less serious felonies.[129] These actions followed the legislative initiatives in the states, as mandatory minimum sentences for drug offenses were already enacted in forty-nine of the fifty states by 1983.[130]

Although Congress began its reenactment of mandatory minimum sentences in 1984, the Anti-Drug Abuse Act of 1986 marked the unquestionable return of the focus of the federal legislature to mandatory minimum sentencing for violations of drug laws. The Anti-Drug Abuse Act of 1986 included provisions that addressed the sales of drugs to persons under

---

122 USSC, 1991:6.
123 USSC, 1991:7.
124 USSC, 1991:7.
125 USC, 1991:8.
126 USSC, 1991:7.
127 21 USC § 860.
128 18 USC § 924 (1).
129 18 USC §3561(b)(1); USSC, 1991:9.
130 USSC, 1991:9.

twenty-one years of age[131] and the employment of persons under eighteen for the commission of offenses that included drugs.[132] Most importantly, the Act provided mandatory minimum sentences for offenses in drug trafficking that were triggered by the amount of drugs involved.[133]

Two years later, Congress enacted the Omnibus Anti-Drug Abuse Act of 1988.[134] This legislative initiative, as discussed previously, singled out crack cocaine from other forms of cocaine and required a term of five years imprisonment for the simple possession of more than five grams of crack cocaine. (The mandatory penalties for continuing a drug enterprise were doubled to twenty years under the Act.[135]) The Anti-Drug Abuse Act of 1988 also applied the same penalties as the underlying substantive act to cases of conspiracy that involve the distribution, importation, or exportation of drugs. All persons convicted in the conspiracy—irrespective of their roles— were required to receive the same sentence as mandated for the substantive offense.[136] During the enactment of the Anti-Drug Abuse Acts of 1986 and 1988, the Sentencing Reform Act was being implemented, and the United States Sentencing Commission was being formed.

The Sentencing Reform Act

In 1984, Congress enacted the Sentencing Reform Act of 1984 (SRA). The SRA provided for the development of the United States Sentencing Commission (USSC). The Congressional intent for the development of the USSC was: (a) to abolish parole and indeterminate sentences; (b) to prevent disparity in sentencing so that similar offenses and offenders would receive similar sentences; and (c) to establish proportionality in sentencing.[137] The USSC was mandated to develop federal sentencing guidelines for the purpose of regulating and bringing consistency to sentencing.[138]

This ushered in a new period of sentencing in federal courts as it limited the potential penalties from which a judge could select in the sentencing of federal defendants, and most importantly, it drastically limited the discretion judges were able to exercise to render sentences they felt were most appropriate on a case by case basis. Prior to the implementation of the SRA, judges were not required to explain their reasons for the sentences they imposed,

---

131 21 USC §859.
132 21 USC 861.
133 21 USC§ 841 (B)(1)(A).
134 21 USC § 844 as amended.
135 21 USC §848(a).
136 USSC, 1991:10.
137 USSC, 1991:16.
138 USSC, 1991:8.

and the sentences were relatively safe from appeal. Additionally, the Parole Commission was the final determiner of the actual amount of time served by the offender, and on the average, the time served was approximately 58 percent of the sentence imposed by the judge. The sentencing process was considered to be "opaque, undocumented, and largely discretionary." There was also the sense that the sentencing process was "unfair, disparate, and ineffective for controlling crime."[139]

The SRA also established the United States Sentencing Commission (USSC) and tasked it with the development of the federal sentencing guidelines. The constitutionality of the USSC and the guidelines were challenged. Consequently, although the guidelines were promulgated in 1987, they were not implemented fully until the Supreme Court's ruling in *Mistretta v. United States*,[140] which held that the USSC and its development of the guidelines were constitutional.

The process used by the USSC in developing the guidelines focused on analyzing one hundred thousand federal sentences imposed in the immediate pre-guidelines era. The Commission determined the average sentence likely to be served for each generic type of crime, and these averages became the "base offense levels" and assisted in establishing the recommended range for imprisonment. Aggravating and mitigating factors that significantly correlated with increases or decreases in sentences were determined statistically, as were their magnitude. These established the "specific offense characteristics" for each type of crime and adjusted the offense level upward or downward. The USSC accounted for offenders' criminal histories in the guidelines as a way to identify offenders most likely to recidivate. The USSC did not rely solely upon the analysis of past sentencing practices for all of the guidelines, as it determined there were compelling reasons to increase the severity of sentences such as those for white-collar crimes and in areas so required by Congress.

SRA and the Anti-Drug Abuse Act of 1986

The ADAA of 1986 required that mandatory minimum penalties of five and ten years be applied to sentences based on the weight of the "mixture or substance containing a detectable amount" of various types of drugs.[141] The USSC reported that determining the correct quantity ratios among different drugs and the correct threshold for each penalty level was problematic.[142]

When Congress passed the ADA of 1986, the USSC was developing

---

139 USSC, November 2004. Fifteen Years of Guidelines Sentencing, iv.
140 488 U.S. 361 (1989).
141 USSC, November 2004, vii.
142 USSC, November 2004.

the initial sentencing guidelines. The USSC incorporated the mandatory minimums into the guidelines and extrapolated upward and downward to establish the guideline ranges for all of the drugs. Offenses involving five or more grams of crack cocaine or five hundred or more grams of powder cocaine received a base offense level of twenty-six which included the guideline range of sixty-three to seventy-eight months for a defendant with a criminal history category of one. In doing so, the applicable range included the mandatory five-year minimum sentence. Similarly, offenses involving fifty or more grams of crack cocaine and five thousand grams or more of powder cocaine, received a base offense level of thirty-two, providing for a sentence within the range of 121 and 151 months for a defendant with a criminal history category of one, and including the required minimum sentence of ten years.[143]

In the end, Congress passed the ADA of 1988, singling out crack cocaine and making it the only drug for which there was a mandatory minimum sentence of five years for simple possession.

The USSC reported the following in several of its reports subsequent to the implementation of the Sentencing Guidelines:

> [R]atios among certain types of drugs contained in the ADAA, and incorporated into the guidelines' Drug Quantity Table, fail in some cases to reflect the relative harmfulness of different drugs. This is particularly true for the 100-to-1 drug quantity ratio between powder and crack cocaine. The quantity thresholds linked to the five- and ten-year sentences for crack cocaine have been shown to result in penalties that are disproportionately long given the relative harmfulness of crack and powder cocaine, and results in lengthy incarceration for many street-level sellers and other low culpability offenders. (USSC, November 2004, pp. vi–vii)

Based upon these findings, the Commission repeatedly recommended to Congress that the mandatory minimum penalty statutes and the guidelines be revised. Beginning with its first report to Congress on federal sentencing policy in 1995, the USSC concluded that Congress's objectives for punishing crack cocaine trafficking could be better accomplished without relying upon the 100:1 quantity ratio. Two years later, in 1997, the USSC again recommended that the 100:1 ratio be changed, which was followed by similar requests in 2002 and 2007.[144]

In their analysis of data from fiscal years 2005 and 2006, the USSC

---

143 Statement of Ricardo H. Hinojosa, Chair, United States Sentencing Commission before the Senate Judiciary Committee Subcommittee on Crime and Drugs.

144 Hinojosa statement.

determined that crack cocaine offenses consistently received substantially longer sentences than powder cocaine offenses. In 2006 the average sentence for crack cocaine offenses was 122 months, and for powder cocaine it was 85 months, representing a 43 percent difference. (In 1992 the difference was approximately 25.3 percent.[145])

Although most cocaine offenders in the federal system are convicted under statutes that mandate a five- or ten-year minimum prison sentence, more crack cocaine offenders (83.0 percent) than powder cocaine offenders (79.1 percent) were subject to these statutes in 2007.[146]

Furthermore, being sentenced under the mandatory minimum sentencing statutes leads to longer average prison sentences, and crack cocaine offenders are less likely to benefit from departure mechanisms, such as safety valves,[147] that were implemented to allow the sentencing of low-level offenders without regard to the statutory mandatory minimums. In 2007 only 13.5 percent of crack cocaine offenders had the safety valve provision applied to their sentences; 44.6 percent of the powder cocaine offenders benefited from this provision.

The mandatory minimum sentencing formulas contained in the Anti-Drug Abuse Acts of 1986 and 1988 had a major impact on the sentencing of women. The role of the offender would no longer be considered in the determination of the sentence, unless it was for the purpose of sentence enhancement. Furthermore, one's family situation, such as being the sole caretaker for minor children, could no longer be considered for the purpose of sentencing. In fact, there was only one method recognized by statute in the 1980s and early 1990s by which a sentence could be less than that which was required by the applicable mandatory minimum sentencing statute, and that was by way of a successful motion of substantial assistance. Subsequently, additional grounds for downward departures were allowed.

Departures

Although some of the stated goals of the Sentencing Guidelines were to eliminate unwarranted disparity, as well as to provide certainty in sentencing, sentences could be imposed that varied from the guidelines. These accepted variances are referred to as departures. There are several types of departures that allow for increasing (upward departures) or lowering (downward departures)

---

145 Hinojosa statement.
146 Hinojosa statement, 5.
147 Safety valve cases may receive either a two-level reduction pursuant to USSG §2D1.1(b)
     (7) and USSG §5C1.2, or relief from the statutory minimum sentence pursuant to 18
     U.S.C. §3553(f), or both.

the sentence outside of the applicable guideline range. The primary departures are:

- Upward departure
- Upward departures with *Booker*
- Above range with *Booker*
  - o §5K1.1 Substantial Assistance
  - o §5K3.1 Early Disposition
- Other Government Sponsored Departures
- Role Adjustments
- Downward Departure
- Safety valves
- Downward Departure with *Booker*
- Below range with *Booker*

Three of the more prevalent departure mechanisms are downward departures for substantial assistance, safety valves, and role adjustments.

— *Substantial Assistance*

The motion for substantial assistance originated through congressional action concurrent with the enactment of the Anti-Drug Abuse Act of 1986. At that time, Congress directed the USSC to provide incentives that would allow downward departures from the provisions of the mandatory sentencing guidelines for offenders who cooperated in the investigation and prosecution of others.[148] The USSC established substantial assistance as a legal mechanism to relax sentencing under the mandatory minimum sentencing scheme through Guideline Policy Statement 5K1.1. A 5K1.1, as it is commonly referred, allows for the reduction of sentences below the mandatory minimum or "guideline range for offenders who assist in the investigation or prosecution of another person committing a criminal offense."[149] The prosecutor considers and presents a 5K1.1 motion to a judge who must decide upon acceptance of the motion and to what extent the sentence should depart from the applicable range of the sentencing guideline or provision for mandatory minimum sentencing. The magnitude of the departure should be determined based

---

148 28 U.S.C. § 994(n).
149 Linda D. Maxfield and John H. Kramer. *Substantial Assistance: An Empirical Yardstick Gauging Equity in Current Federal Policy and Practice.* (Washington, DC: USSC, 1998), 2.

upon the degree and nature of the defendant's cooperation.[150] Although legally irrelevant, factors such as gender, race, education, and ethnicity, have been reported to influence the degree of the §5K1.1 departure. Female defendants have been shown to benefit more from the use of departure than males, and whites more so than minorities.[151]

— Safety Valves

The *safety valve* provides a mechanism by which only drug offenders who meet certain statutory criteria may be sentenced without regard to the otherwise applicable mandatory minimum provisions. Enacted in 1994, the safety valve provision was created by Congress to permit offenders "who are the least culpable participants in drug trafficking offenses, to receive strictly regulated reductions in prison sentences for mitigating factors recognized in the federal sentencing guidelines."[152] Safety valve cases may receive either a 2-level reduction pursuant to USSG §2D1.1(b)(7) and USSG §5C1.2, or relief from the statutory minimum sentence pursuant to 18 U.S.C. §3553(f), or both.

— Role Adjustments

Role adjustments are part of the sentencing guidelines. These provisions[153] allow the sentencing judge to either increase or decrease an offender's offense level by two to four levels based upon the court's determination of whether mitigating or aggravating circumstances warrant such adjustments. Reductions may be implemented for a mitigating role in situations when the offender's role was "minimal or minor (or between minimal and minor)."[154] The USSC reported that between 1996 and 2006, mitigating role reductions were applied to offenses involving powdered cocaine at rates two to three times higher than offenses involving crack cocaine.[155]

Source of Disparity under the Guidelines

The USSC determined that the Guidelines have had a positive effect in increasing transparency and predictability of sentences that fall under the guidelines. Furthermore, although the SRA focused on sentencing, the USSC

---

150 Maxfield and Kramer, 1998, 17.
151 Maxfield and Kramer, 1998, 19.
152 Hinojosa statement, 5.
153 USSG §3B1.1(increase) and USSG §3B1.2 (decrease).
154 USSC, May 2007. p. 39 footnote 47.
155 USSC, May 2007. p. 41.

and Congress, as well as others, realized that disparity may be impacted by presentencing actions of the attorney general, such as the decision to bring charges, decline prosecution, dismiss a case, or offer plea bargains. Congress tasked the USSC to monitor and evaluate plea bargaining and its impact on disparity. It is much more difficult to complete a quantitative analysis of the disparity in the presentencing process as minimal data exist; the process is still very much a black box for which there is little or no transparency or records to explain what underlies the decisions made during the presentencing process. The USSC reported in 2004 that "the mechanisms and procedures designed to control disparity arising at presentencing stages are not all working as intended and have not been adequate to fully achieve uniformity of sentencing."[156]

Plea bargaining continues to introduce disparity into the federal criminal justice system. The USSC, in 1989, 1995, and 2000, compared descriptions of the offense conduct contained in samples of presenting reports with the conduct for which offenders were ultimately charged and sentenced. Each time, numerous qualifying offenders were found not to have been charged with potentially applicable penalty statutes. The resultant charges included some that were above what the guidelines would require, while others resulted in the offenders being charged at guideline ranges that were less than what appropriately reflected their actions. The USSC determined that the sentences were disproportionate to the seriousness of the offense and disparate among offenders who engaged in similar conduct.[157]

The USSC also determined that departures—both the rate and the extent of departures—are a source of disparity within the federal criminal justice system. Departures for substantial assistance underlie the largest variation of sentence lengths, as discovered by the USSC. The variation accounted for 4.4 percent in sentence length. Other downward departures only accounted for 2.2 percent, and upward departures contributed to just 0.29 percent of the variation in sentence length. The rate of substantial assistance and other downward departures was found by the USSC to be similar—17.1 percent and 18.3 percent, respectively. Substantial assistance departures account for more variability in sentence length because on average the extent of departure for substantial assistance is greater.[158]

The SRA provides for an automatic right-of-appeal if a judge imposes a sentence that is not within the prescribed guideline range.[159] If the sentence is higher than the range, the defendant may appeal; if it is lower than the range,

156   USSC. Fifteen Years of Guidelines Sentencing. (Washington, DC: U.S. Government Printing Office, November 2004) xii.
157   USSC, November 2004, p. xii.
158   USSC, November 2004, p. xiii.
159   18 U.S.C. §3742.

the government may appeal. The alleged misapplication of the guidelines is grounds for either party to appeal.

In 1987, Congress established that:

> The court shall impose a sentence of the kind, and within the range [required by the guidelines] unless the court finds that there exists an aggravating or mitigating circumstance of a kind, or to a degree, not adequately taken into consideration by the Sentencing Commission in formulating the guidelines that should result in a sentence different from that described. (18 U.S.C § 3553(b)).

Just how restrictive the standard for departure was to be cannot be determined by the legislative record. Representative John Conyers, in authoring the amendment, appears to have intended to expand the discretion of the sentencing judge to enable him or her to depart from the guidelines. A joint explanation was included in the Congressional Record by several senators, but this insertion contradicts the intentions of Rep. Conyers.[160] Consequently, the USSC, the courts, and the legislature informed the practice of whether the guidelines were presumptive, mandatory, or a bit of both. In June 2004, the Supreme Court decided *Blakely v. Washington*.[161] Prior to that decision, it was commonly agreed that the guidelines were not voluntary; departures could be applied if there were reasons for doing so that would withstand appellate review. The degree to which the guidelines were mandatory was in dispute. In 2003, Congress determined that there were far too many departures from the sentencing guidelines and enacted the PROTECT Act of 2003; among other things, the act implemented *de novo* review upon appeal of downward departures. PROTECT also required the USSC to significantly reduce the incidences of downward departures by amending the guidelines and policy statements. Amendment 651 by the USSC adhered to these Congressional dictates and narrowed the circumstances in which departure is authorized. The court's decisions in *Blakely v. Washington*[162] and later *United States v. Booker*[163] confirmed that the guidelines were advisory and not mandatory.

Powdered Cocaine and Crack Cocaine

In order to appreciate the nature of the public policies regarding each of these

---

160 Marc Miller and Ronald Wright. "Your Cheatin' Heart(land): The Long Search for Administrative Sentencing Justice." *Buffalo Criminal Law Review* 2.
161 124 S.Ct. 2531 (June 24, 2004).
162 124 S.Ct. 2531 (June 24, 2004).
163 543 U.S. 220 (205).

substances, it is important to develop an understanding of what constitutes crack cocaine and powdered cocaine. Although there were very few research findings available on the differentiation between these substances when the Anti-Drug Abuse Acts of 1986 and 1988 were enacted, the current state of knowledge is bountiful with information.

Cocaine is a naturally occurring substance and is derived from the leaves of exythroxylon plants that grow in South America. Crack cocaine is a product of powdered cocaine. Cocaine has been used in South America for more than three thousand years and in the United States since the early nineteenth century.[164] Powdered cocaine is smuggled into the United States primarily from Colombia, Mexico, and the Caribbean nations, and then through Arizona, southern California, southern Florida, and Texas. Large shipments of over twenty-five kilograms are usually brought through Houston, Los Angeles, Miami, and New York City.[165] Crack is manufactured from the imported cocaine in local neighborhoods of the United States, where most retail sales in urban areas are performed by poor minority youth under age eighteen, who sell crack and cocaine for profit. In urban areas the drugs are sold on street corners, in open-air markets, by freelancers and runners, and in houses.[166] Most policing strategies and research regarding crack has focused on its use, proliferation, and containment in urban areas. As a result, there is little information about how crack or cocaine is sold in suburban and upper-class neighborhoods or to professional businesspeople.[167]

Cocaine is both a potent anesthetic and a powerful stimulant. In the United States, cocaine was used in elixirs for depression as well as other symptoms. It was used as an ingredient in cigars, cigarettes, chewing gum, tonics, and Coca-Cola.[168] In 1906, although the population of the United States was approximately half of what it is today, the population consumed as much cocaine as did the population in 1976.[169] In 1914 the Harrison Act banned the use of cocaine for nonmedicinal purposes. Consequently, the drug became quite scarce. In the 1960s, cocaine reappeared as an illicit substance that readily led to abusive use.[170]

Cocaine is the most potent naturally occurring stimulant of the central nervous system. The physiological effects of cocaine include alertness and

---

164 John P. Morgan and Lynn Zimmer. "The Social Pharmacology of Smokeable Cocaine." *Crack in America*. Ed. Craig Reinarman and Henry Levine. (Berkeley, CA: University Press, 1997); USSC, 1995:7.

165 USSC, 1995.

166 Morgan and Zimmer, 1997; USSC, 1995.

167 USSC, 1995, 66–70.

168 Morgan and Zimmer, 1997; USSC, 1995, 8.

169 USSC, 1995, 8.

170 Morgan and Zimmer, 1997.

heightened energy. The psychotropic effects of cocaine include a sense of euphoria, decreased anxiety and social inhibitions, and heightened sexuality. Increasing the cocaine dosages and using rapid methods for administrating the drug produce euphoric experiences and create vivid, long-term psychological memories that lead to craving for the drug. Psychosis and hallucinations may occur if the doses of cocaine are increased further. Increased dosage also creates craving for other drugs such as alcohol.[171]

It is important to note that the different forms of cocaine do not produce different physiological or psychotropic effects; rather, the method of administration impacts the immediacy, intensity, and duration of the effects of cocaine.[172] Furthermore, cocaine is not physiologically addictive, as are opiates, heroin, barbiturates, nicotine, caffeine, and alcohol. Rather, cocaine is psychologically addictive because it creates a compulsion for repeated use that results from its euphoric effects.[173]

The route of administration that most rapidly increases the concentration of the substance in the blood system will maximize the level of psychotropic effect. The greater the intensity of the drug's effects, the shorter their duration. Injecting or smoking the drug will provide the fastest onset of effects with a short period of duration; the result is that this type of user will administer the drug more frequently than one who snorts or ingests the drug because the latter user experiences a slower onset and longer duration of the effects.[174]

The final form of the drug determines how it will be used as well as the intensity and duration of the physiological and psychotropic effects.[175] The various forms include leaves, paste, powder, and base. Freebase and crack are derived from the base form of cocaine. The coco leaves are 0.1 to 0.8 percent pure. Paste is an intermediate product of the process of making cocaine. Powdered cocaine is derived by dissolving the paste in hydrochloric acid and water and adding such things as potassium salt, ammonia, sugars, or benzocaine, to dilute the mixture. The purity of powdered cocaine varies. Cocaine base is cocaine alkaloid that is "freed" from salt substrate and is similar to paste. Dissolving powdered cocaine in water and ammonia and then adding ether or an organic solvent results in freebase. Crack is a form of cocaine base derived from powdered cocaine. The powdered cocaine is dissolved in a solution of sodium bicarbonate substance and water. It is then boiled, and the solids crystallize and separate. The solid substance (the residual crystals) is crack cocaine. It is broken into "rocks" equaling 0.1 to 0.5 gram.

---

171 Morgan and Zimmer, 1997; USSC, 1995, 19–20.
172 Morgan and Zimmer, 1997; USSC, 1995, 19.
173 Morgan and Zimmer, 1997.
174 Morgan and Zimmer, 1997; USSC, 1995, 20–24.
175 USSC, 1995, 7.

Crack cocaine is 10 to 40 percent pure cocaine by weight.[176] One gram of pure powdered cocaine equals 0.89 gram of crack.[177]

The smoking of cocaine (crack cocaine) has not been proven to be more addictive than the snorting of cocaine (powdered cocaine).[178]

Cocaine Drug Quantity and Dosages

Based upon the Anti-Drug Abuse Acts of 1986 and 1988, the primary determinates of sentence or offense levels are the type and amount of drug. In 2006 the median drug weight for powder cocaine was 6,000 grams; for crack cocaine offenses it was 51 grams. In 2007 a preliminary analysis indicated that the median weights had increased to 6,240 grams for powder cocaine and 53.5 grams for crack cocaine offenses.[179] To understand the impact of these quantities on use, it is important to understand that one gram of powder cocaine yields approximately five to ten doses and one gram of crack cocaine produces about two to ten doses. In comparison, the five hundred grams of powder cocaine that is required to initiate the five-year statutory mandatory minimum prison sentence will yield between 2,500 and 5,000 doses, as compared to the five grams of crack cocaine that triggers the same penalty and yields from ten to fifty doses.[180]

Cocaine and Offender Conduct

The USSC determined that only a "minority" of powder or crack cocaine offenders involve weapons, violence, or an aggravating role in the offense. Although such involvement is more prevalent in offenses involving crack cocaine, "the presence in both offenses occurs in less than seven percent of the cases."[181] Furthermore, the occurrence of violence has decreased for both powder and crack cocaine since 2002. In 2005 the USSC determined that 93.8 percent of powder cocaine offenses and 89.6 percent of crack offenses involved *no* violence. Deaths occurred in 1.6 percent of the powder cocaine cases and 2.2 percent of the crack cocaine cases. Any injury whatsoever occurred in 1.5 percent of the powder cocaine cases and 3.3 percent of the crack cocaine cases,

---

176 Morgan and Zimmer, 1997.
177 USSC, 1995, 11–14.
178 Morgan and Zimmer, 1997.
179 Hinojosa statement, 9.
180 United States Sentencing Commission. *Report to the Congress: Cocaine and Federal Sentencing Policy.* (Washington, DC: US Government Printing Office, May 2007) 63.
181 Hinojosa statement, 10.

while the threat of violence was associated with 3.2 percent of the powder cocaine cases and 4.9 percent of the crack cocaine cases.[182]

The Adverse Impact of the 100:1 Powder-to-Cocaine Ratio

In 2002, 81 percent of the offenders sentenced for trafficking crack cocaine were African American.[183] The average length of imprisonment for crack cocaine was one hundred nineteen months, compared to seventy-eight months for the powder form of the drug. Average sentences for crack cocaine were twenty-five months longer than for methamphetamine and eighty-one months longer than for heroin.[184] The reason for the harsher treatment of crack cocaine offenses is the low threshold amounts for the five- and ten-year mandatory minimum sentences that are built into the mandatory minimum penalty statutes and incorporated into the Drug Quantity Table of the guidelines. Crack cocaine is the only drug for which simple possession of greater than five grams, even without an intent to distribute, is treated the same as drug trafficking.[185]

Beginning in 1995, the USSC repeatedly recommended that Congress and the sitting president increase the threshold amount for crack cocaine that triggered mandatory minimum sentencing. The recommendation has yet to be adhered to, although various federal legislators have submitted several bills.

The USSC made the following recommendations to a congressional subcommittee on February 12, 2008:

- The Commission believes that there is no justification for the current statutory penalty scheme for powder and crack cocaine. The Commission remains committed, however, to its recommendation in 2002 that any statutory ratio be no more than 20-to-1. Specifically, consistent with its May 2007 Report, the Commission strongly and unanimously recommends that Congress:

    o Increase the five- year and ten-year statutory mandatory minimum threshold quantities for crack cocaine to focus the penalties more closely on serious and major traffickers as described generally in the legislative history of the 1986 Act.

---

182 USSC, May 2007 Report, 38; Fig 2-20.
183 United States Sentencing Commission. *Sourcebook of Federal Sentencing Statistics.* (Washington, DC: US Government Printing Office, 2002) Table 34.
184 USSC, 2002, Figure J.
185 USSC, November 2004, 131–132.

o Repeal the mandatory minimum penalty provision for simple possession of crack cocaine under 21 U.S.C. §844.

• Reject addressing the 100-to 1 drug quantity ratio by decreasing the five-year and ten-year statutory mandatory minimum threshold quantities for powder cocaine offenses, as there is no evidence to justify such an increase in quantity-based penalties for powder cocaine offenses.[186]

Demographics and Cocaine

According to the USSC, in 2006 African Americans continued to comprise the majority of crack cocaine offenders convicted in the federal system, although their percentages decreased by almost 10 percent from 1992 to 2006 (91.4 percent and 81.8 percent, respectively). The percentage of white crack cocaine offenders increased from 3.2 percent to 8.8 percent over the same time. In 2006 the demographics of powder cocaine offenders had also shifted, with the majority group being Hispanic (57.5 percent), followed by African American (27.0 percent) and white (14.3 percent) offenders. [187]

Racial, Ethnic, and Gender Disparity and the Sentencing Guidelines

Prior to the implementation of the SRA, most of the federal offenders were white. Presently, minorities, particularly Hispanics and African Americans, comprise the majority of federal prisoners. Prior to the guidelines, the differences between average sentences for whites and minorities was relatively small, but the gap between African Americans and other racial and ethnic groups began to increase due to the implementation of the ADAA of 1986 and 1988, both of which required mandatory minimum sentences for drug offenses. [188]

Disparity, Discrimination, and Adverse Impacts

The USSC defines unwarranted disparity as:

[D]ifferent treatment of *individual* offenders who are similar in relevant ways, or similar treatment of *individual* offenders who differ in characteristics that are relevant to the purposes of sentencing.... As long as the individuals in each [demographic] group are treated

---

186 Hinojosa statement, 11.
187 USSC 2007, 16, Table 2-1.
188 USSC, November 2004, xiv.

fairly, average group differences simply reflect differences in the characteristics of the individuals who comprise each group. Group disparity is not necessarily unwarranted disparity.[189]

The SRA requires that the sentencing guidelines and policy statements are "entirely neutral as to the race, sex, national origin, creed, and socioeconomic status of offenders."[190] Different treatment based on these factors is unwarranted disparity that is defined as discrimination. Discrimination may be conscious or unconscious, based upon stereotypes or fears of particular groups of people, or a preference for certain people because of the group to which they belong. The guidelines were developed to do away with discrimination in sentencing.

The USSC, in its report to Congress in 1995, highlighted another category of concern that threatened fairness in sentencing. The USSC stated, "If a sentencing rule had a disproportionate impact on a particular demographic group, however unintentional, it raises special concerns about whether the rule is a necessary and effective means to achieve the purposes of sentencing."[191]

Speaking specifically to the 100:1 ratio of powdered cocaine to crack cocaine that resulted in identical penalties, the USSC advised:

> Congress chose to more severely penalize those dealing in crack cocaine because of a perception that crack had proven particularly harmful.… [T]he high percentage of Blacks convicted of crack cocaine offenses is a matter of great concern.… [W]hen such an enhanced ratio for a particular form of drug has a disproportionate effect on one segment of the population, it is particularly important that sufficient policy bases exist in support of the enhanced ratio. (USSC, 1995, p.xii)[192]

The War on Drugs Twenty Years Later: *United States v. Booker*[193]

On January 12, 2005, the United States Supreme Court held that the provisions that made the sentencing guidelines mandatory were invalid, thus establishing that the guidelines were to be seen as advisory only. In the court's opinion, as written by Justice Stevens, it was determined that, although the guidelines allow for departures from the designated sentencing range in matters where the judge "finds that there exists an aggravating or mitigating

---

189 USSC, November 2004, 113.
190 28 U.S.C.§994(d).
191 USSC, November 2004, p. 114.
192 USSC, 2004, 114.
193 543 U.S. 220 (2005).

circumstance of a kind, or a degree, not adequately taken into consideration by the Sentencing Commission in formulating the guidelines that should result in a sentence different from that described,"[194] this does not make them advisory. As indicated by the court, departures are not available in most cases, and because in most cases the USSC would have taken all relevant factors into account, the test for allowing a departure from the guidelines would not exist. The judge would therefore be required to impose a sentence within the range prescribed by the guidelines, thus making them mandatory and in violation of the sixth amendment's guarantee to a jury trial.[195]

USSC's Amendment Regarding Penalties for Crack Cocaine

In 2007 the USSC exercised its authority and amended the Federal Sentencing Guidelines to reduce the penalties for crack cocaine. The Commission's amendment took effect on November 1, 2007. The amendment was "intended as a step toward reducing some of the unwarranted disparity currently existing between Federal crack cocaine and powder cocaine sentences."[196] The amendment was made retroactively effective to March 3, 2008. The USSC made it clear, however, that any comprehensive response to the adverse impacts of the federal sentencing penalties for crack cocaine offense would still require legislation by Congress that revised the current statutory penalties.[197]

194   18 U.S.C.A. §3553(b)(1) (Supp.2004).

195   The Supreme Court also held in *United States v. Booker* that any fact (other than a prior conviction) which is necessary to support a sentence exceeding the maximum authorized by the facts established by a guilty plea or jury verdict must be admitted by the defendant or proved to a jury beyond a reasonable doubt.

196   News Release, USSC, December 11, 2007.

197   Hinojosa statement.

CHAPTER FIVE

Investigating the Impact of the War on Drugs on the Incarceration of Black Women at the Federal Level

---

Marsha C. – Fifteen Years for Crack Conspiracy[198]

Marsha received a 190-month sentence as a nonviolent, first-time offender. She was convicted of possession with intent to distribute cocaine base and cocaine, and aiding and abetting. At the time of the offense, she was twenty-six years old, had a good job with a mortgage company, lived in a condo, and had paid for one of her two vehicles. Then she fell in love with a man whom she allowed to move in with her. She thought her life was moving in the right direction.

On August 5, 1997, Marsha returned home and was greeted by DEA agents. They told her that her boyfriend had been arrested for drug trafficking. After the agents found drugs in the storage compartment in her stove, she, too, was arrested. Marsha's position was that she knew nothing about the drugs, nor where her boyfriend got them. One FBI agent told her that he believed she did not know about the drugs being in the stove but felt she had some idea of where her boyfriend had gotten them from; Marsha had no information to share. Because of her association with her boyfriend, and because he lived with her and drove her car, Marsha was found guilty of the same crime for which he was convicted: possession with intent to distribute cocaine and cocaine base. Marsha indicates that the FBI made no other connections between her and the drugs—no selling on her part, no sales in her home, no telephone calls, and no transactions in her presence.

Sentence: fifteen years for crack conspiracy

---

198   http://november.org/thewall/cases/cunningham-m/cunningham-m.html. 11/27/2009.

The analysis of data is an important way by which to add to our understanding of how the war on drugs impacts the incarceration of women— and black women specifically—in the federal system. As an attorney and former legislator, I know firsthand how policies and laws impact people and groups. As a researcher, I appreciate the tools provided by data and statistics to get even more in-depth answers to if, how, and why the drug laws have impacted the likelihood of incarceration and the length of prison sentences received by black women convicted of drug offenses involving crack cocaine. In this chapter I establish the groundwork for the statistical analyses that follow in the next two chapters and that will ground the discussion of drug policies and black women.

Although many states enacted laws regarding crack cocaine that are punitive relative to the laws established for other types of drugs, no state has a drug policy that is more punitive than the federal system.[199] This chapter will examine how the federal drug policies for crack cocaine have impacted the incarceration of black women. Some of the analyses include white and Hispanic women in order to provide information about their imprisonment in the federal system for drugs offenses. This inquiry centers on black women, however, and will review the effects of the drug policies for crack cocaine on their incarceration.

Why Focus on the Federal System?

The federal system is selected for a number of important reasons. First, the Anti-Drug Abuse Acts of 1986 and 1988 established solid parameters for the war on drugs at the federal level. Second, the controversy surrounding the 100:1 ratio established by the federal government has seldom included a discussion of black females. Third, although many states have included mandatory minimum sentencing for drugs, particularly crack cocaine, none have enacted drug policies as punitive as those of the federal system.[200] Fourth, state prosecutors often have the option to prosecute drug offenses in their jurisdictions in state courts or to forward the cases to the federal attorneys for prosecution at the federal level. Finally, the federal system, along with California and Texas, houses more than one-third of all female prisoners in the United States.[201] Consequently, the findings regarding the federal system can provide important information with the potential to impact the social and fiscal costs of the war on drugs and to inform policy at the federal and state levels.

---

199 USSC, 1995.
200 USSC, 1995.
201 BJS, 2008. Prisoners in 2007 (Washington, DC) Appendix Table 2.

Defining the War on Drugs

This analysis defines the war on drugs as the mandatory minimum sentencing schemes applied to drug offenses involving crack cocaine established in the Anti-Drug Abuse Acts of 1986 and 1988. These statutes prescribe mandatory minimum sentences that require the incarceration of persons convicted of the simple possession of crack cocaine, as well as low-level dealing, manufacturing, trafficking, and conspiracy. At least twenty-three years after their initial enactment, these laws had not been repealed or modified substantially, although there have been some modifications, such as downward departures. Additionally, even if the laws are changed, there will still be thousands of black women who have been or remain incarcerated under these laws.

The Data

The United States Sentencing Commission (USSC) collected the data used in this study.[202] The data sets include information for all federal cases sentenced from October 1, 1995, to September 30, 1996 (FY1996 and hereinafter referred to as 1996), and October 1, 2005, to September 30, 2006 (FY2006 and hereinafter referred to as 2006), under the Sentencing Guidelines and Policy Statements of the Sentencing Reform Act of 1984, for which information was submitted to the USSC. The goal of the study was to test the impact that the war on drugs has had on black women convicted of drug offenses in the federal system. Data from 1996 and 2006, one and two decades, respectively, after the enactment of the Anti-Drug Abuse Act of 1986, provided the opportunity to compare the impact ten and twenty years after the initial enactment of the war on drugs.

The population from which the sample was selected included 42,436 cases for 1996 and 71,014 for 2006. The samples for the research consisted of all cases that involved black, white, and Hispanic females, who were sentenced in jurisdictions of the federal court for drug offenses as their primary sentencing offense during 1996 and 2006 and for whom there was sufficient information for each of the selected variables. When analyses by types of drug were made, for example crack cocaine, cases were selected for which the *primary* drug

---

202 Monitoring Of Federal Criminal Statutes, 1987–1996 [1995–1996. DATA] [Computer file]. ICPSR version. Washington, D.C.: U.S. Sentencing Commission [producer], 1996. Ann Arbor, MI: Inter-University Consortium for Political and social Research (distributor), 1999.

offense for which the women were sentenced involved crack cocaine.[203] The unit of analysis was the individual cases.[204]

— *Variables*

The primary independent variables (that is, factors expected to have an impact on the likelihood of incarceration of length of prison sentence received based upon prior research) used in the study are: demographic group, criminal history, drug mandatory minimum sentencing, drug amount in grams, departure from mandatory minimum sentencing, and the interaction between drug mandatory minimum sentencing and drug type. The dependent variables (the outcomes) were: (a) the imposition of a mandatory minimum sentence at zero, five, or ten years, (b) prison in/out, and (c) total length of prison sentence or the natural log of length of prison sentence. Other variables that were considered to be of substantive significance in the sentencing of females were also included in the analyses. These variables included: age of defendant at sentencing, number of defendant's dependents, downward departure from statute, role adjustment, and level of education completed. Additional information about the variables and a table of all of the variables can be found in Appendix A.

The Primary Research Questions

The research questions were informed by the review of prior research and include factors (i.e., the independent variables including type of drug, drug mandatory minimum sentence, the interaction between drug type and mandatory minimum sentence, prior criminal history, amount of drugs, departure from mandatory minimum, and type of drug offense) that are expected to influence the outcomes (i.e., dependent variables, which are the imposition of mandatory minimum sentences, if a woman was sentenced to prison, and the length of prison sentence imposed). The primary questions are:

Primary Question One:
What influence did crack cocaine and downward departures have on the

---

203　If the primary offense for which they were sentenced was not for drugs or a particular type of drug, then they were not included in the sample. Therefore, there were many other women who were convicted and sentenced in 1996 and 2006 for drug offenses involving crack cocaine, but they were not included because they don't meet these criteria.

204　The data regarding women of other racial and ethnic groups, such as Alaskan/Inuit, Native Americans, Asian, Pacific Islanders, is not included in the study because they are so few in number within the data set.

sentencing of black females who were convicted of drug offenses that required a mandatory minimum sentence?

Primary Question Two:

Did the influences of crack cocaine and downward departures on the sentencing of black females for drug offenses involving crack change between 1996 and 2006?

Working Research Questions

The following research questions were used to test the impact of the various factors, or variables, that are contained within the Anti-Drug Abuse Acts of 1986 and 1988, as well as the mechanisms for departure from the mandatory sentences prescribed by the Anti-Drug Abuse Acts. Consistent with the entire study, the primary focus of the questions was to test the impact of the mandatory minimum sentences for crack cocaine on the incarceration of black females convicted of drug offenses. For some research questions, I discuss findings about the impact of various variables on all women (black, white, and Hispanic) who were convicted of drug offenses. I felt this was important in order to indicate how the various groups are impacted similarly or differently.

All of the analyses of the research questions took into consideration the type of drug (specifically crack cocaine as compared to all other types of drugs in general or powdered cocaine specifically),[205] prior record, the amount of drugs, as well as other variables that are of substantive significance (acceptance of responsibility, downward departure, age, number of dependents, level of education). For each research question, the impact of the variable was analyzed for 1996 and 2006, and a comparison of the two years was then made to determine if a change appeared to have occurred between the two time periods. Additionally, the impact of the application of downward departures was also analyzed for the two time periods, 1996 and 2006. Levels of significance were at $p < .05$.

The working research questions were as follows:

Question One

Did being convicted of drug offenses involving crack cocaine increase the odds that mandatory minimum sentences of five or ten years would be imposed in cases that involved (a) all women and (b) black females? How did the two years compare to each other?

Question Two

Did being convicted of drug offenses involving crack cocaine increase the

---

205   When a drug is specified, it is the primary drug for which woman was convicted.

likelihood of incarceration for all women? How did the two years compare to each other?

Question Three

Did being convicted of drug offenses involving crack cocaine increase the lengths of prison sentences for all women? How did the two years compare to each other?

Question Four

Did being convicted of drug offenses involving crack cocaine increase the lengths of prison sentences for black females? How did the two years compare to each other?

Question Five

Did mandatory minimum sentencing increase the amount of prison time received by black females who were convicted of drug offenses involving crack cocaine? What impact, if any, did their prior records, amount of drugs involved in the offenses, role adjustments, or the application of downward departure have on the sentences? How did the two years compare to each other?

Question Six

Did mandatory minimum sentencing increase the likelihood that women who were sentenced for drug offenses involving crack cocaine would receive prison sentences? What impact, if any, did the application of downward departure have on the sentences? How did the two years compare to each other?

Question Seven

Did mandatory minimum sentencing increase the likelihood that women who were convicted of drug offenses involving drugs other than crack cocaine would receive prison sentences? What impact, if any, did the application of downward departure have on the sentences? How did the two years compare to each other?

Question Eight

Did mandatory minimum sentencing increase the likelihood of receiving prison sentences among black females who were sentenced for drug offenses in which crack cocaine was the primary drug? What impact, if any, did the application of downward departure have on the sentences? What impact, if any, did the prior records of the women or the amount of drugs involved, have on the likelihood that the women would receive prison sentences? How did the two years compare to each other?

Question Nine

Did being convicted of a drug offense involving crack cocaine as compared to powder cocaine increase the likelihood that a woman would receive (a) a five-year or (b) a ten-year sentence? How do the findings compare between 1996 and 2006?

Analysis Techniques

The data were analyzed using both descriptive and multivariate techniques. The descriptive analyses provided an idea of what happened, whereas the multivariate analyses provided some idea of why it happened.[206] The following chapters present the findings.

---

206 The multivariate analyses of the data consist of logistic regressions and linear regressions. Specifically, logistic regression is used to test the influence of the independent variables on logit odds of the dichotomous dependent variables: (1) imposition of mandatory minimum sentences at zero, five, or ten years; and, (2) prison in/out. Multiple linear regressions are conducted to test the impact of various independent variables on the length of prison sentences and the natural log of the length of prison sentences.

CHAPTER SIX

Investigating What Happened:
Descriptive Analyses of the Data

Tonya D. – Ten-Year Mandatory Minimum Sentence for Possession with Intent to Distribute Crack Cocaine[207]

In 1990, Tonya was a single mother of four trying to help her family survive on the assistance she received through Aid to Families with Dependent Children. That summer at a swap meet she encountered Fred, an acquaintance from the neighborhood. Fred asked Tonya to mail a package for him to his brother whose birthday was the next day. Fred gave Tonya a one-hundred-dollar bill and told her to keep the change. Was she suspicious? Yes, but Tonya indicated that she needed the money for her kids, so she decided to mail the package.

The security guard at the mailing facility at the airport became suspicious of Tonya because she appeared to be nervous. The guard wrote down her license plate number, and when she left, he and the other workers opened the package. It was determined that it contained 232 grams of crack cocaine. The LAPD interrogated Tonya, and she told them what had happened. The act was considered a federal offense because of the amount of drugs involved. Tonya was given a mandatory minimum sentence of ten years and did not receive a reduction in sentence based upon substantial assistance because Fred died shortly after her arrest.

Sentence: ten-year mandatory minimum sentence for possession with intent to distribute crack cocaine

---

207 http://www/hr95.org/Drake,T.html. 11/27/2009.

The war on drugs, with the focus on crack cocaine, began in 1986 with the enactment of the Anti-Drug Abuse Act of 1986 (ADAA). Now more than twenty years later, although the Act itself has not been changed, there have been significant measures instituted that allow for the imposition of sentences that are lower than the mandatory minimums required by the ADAAs of 1986 and 1988.

Research indicates that in the latter part of the 1980s and the early 1990s, white, black, and Hispanic women were impacted by the mandatory minimums set forth for various drugs. This chapter will review and compare the incarceration of women in the federal system in 1996 and 2006. As demonstrated by many of the studies discussed previously, descriptive analyses provide important information about the variables and their associations with other important variables. In this chapter, the results of descriptive analyses concerning key variables (types of offenses, types of drugs, demographic groups, mandatory minimum sentences, amount of drugs, and prior record) are reported. The population and the sample are also depicted descriptively. Associations between the demographic groups and (1) type of sentence received, (2) length of sentence imposed, (3) prior records, and (4) types of drugs involved in the convictions are investigated. These variables were selected because they have been shown by previous research to be relevant factors used in sentencing.

Descriptive analyses enable us to get an understanding of what is happening in various situations. The primary questions guiding this descriptive review are:

1. What are the types of offenses for which women were convicted and sentenced in the federal system in 1996 and 2006?

2. What were the primary drugs involved in the drug offenses for which the women were convicted and sentenced?

3. What percentage of women convicted of drug offenses were convicted under mandatory minimum sentencing laws?

4. What were the prior criminal record levels of the women?

5. What were the amounts of drugs involved in the drug offenses?

6. What was the relationship between crack cocaine and the incarceration of black women in 1996 and 2006? Based upon the descriptive analysis of the data, what changes do we observe and what questions are we left with regarding the evolution of the war on drugs and Black women?

Where appropriate, the investigation disaggregated the women into the three racial/ethnic groups most found in the federal system (white, black, and Hispanic) in order to determine if the relationships between the variables differed among the three groups of women.

In this study, mandatory minimum sentencing is an integral element in the working definition or operationalization of the concept of the war on drugs. To more clearly understand the relationship between mandatory minimum sentences received by the women in this sample, several descriptive analyses are included that focus on mandatory minimum sentences for drug offenses and their associations with the demographic groups, types of drug offenses, types of drugs involved in the offenses, and the decision to imprison. This chapter concludes with a section that focuses specifically on black women who are convicted of offenses that involve crack.

The analysis of these key variables is the first step in the investigation of the relationships between demographic groups, mandatory minimum sentences, types of drugs, the decision to imprison, and the length of incarceration. These analyses provide important information that is fundamental to the investigation of the impact of the war on drugs on women in general and on black females specifically. These investigations provide the framework within which the multivariate analyses can proceed.

Descriptive Analysis

In 1996, there were 6,114 black, white, and Hispanic females in the population of women convicted of offenses in federal court and for whom information was sent to the USSC for fiscal year 1996. Of this group, 34 percent were black, 44 percent were white, and 22 percent were Hispanic. The primary offenses for which these women were convicted were "other offenses" (38.4 percent), drug offenses (34.8 percent), and property offenses (19.2 percent). The category for "other offenses" included the violation of laws that concern civil rights, immigration, pornography and prostitution, offenses while in prison, and offenses related to the administration of justice; environment, game, and fish; national defense; food and drug; traffic; and other miscellaneous statutes. The category "drug offense" constituted the single largest homogeneous group of offenses for which women were incarcerated in the federal system. Ten years later, in 2006, the total number of women convicted in federal court had increased to 8,519. Of this group, 26.4 percent were black (down by 8 percent), 40.8 percent were white (down by 3.2 percent) and 32.8 percent were Hispanic (up by 10.8 percent). The primary offenses for which the women were convicted in 2006 in federal court were: drugs (35.8 percent), economic offenses (32.1 percent), and other (20.6 percent). Within this ten-year period, drug offenses had taken the lead among the offenses for which women were convicted in the federal court system.[208]

208 ICPSR 9317–FY96 and ICPSR 20120-FY06.

In 1996, among the 2,130 black, white, and Hispanic women for whom a drug offense was the primary charge underlying their conviction, 34.2 percent were black, 33.4 percent were white, and 32.4 percent were Hispanic. Considering that black females comprised only 12.4 percent of the uninstitutionalized female population, they were represented disproportionately (by a factor of three) among all incarcerated females as well as among females who were incarcerated for drug offenses.

Among the 3,250 black, white, and Hispanic women for whom a drug offense was the primary charge for their conviction in 2006, 19 percent were black, 41.6 percent were white, and 39.3 percent were Hispanic. Thus, there was a significant decrease (-15.4 percent) in the amount of black women from 1996 to 2006, but an increase in the percentages of white (8.2 percent) and Hispanic (7.9 percent) females among women who were convicted of drug offenses in the federal system.

Between 1996 and 2006, the type of drug involved in women's drug offenses also changed significantly. Among the women who were convicted of drug offenses in the federal system for 1996, the primary drugs involved were powdered cocaine, crack cocaine, and marijuana (see Table 6.1). By 2006 the primary drugs were methamphetamines, marijuana, and powdered cocaine.

Table 6.1: Types of Drugs for which Women Were Convicted and Sentenced, 1996, 2006

Drug Type	Number of Women 1996 2006	Percentage of Women 1996 2006	% Change 1996–2006
Powdered cocaine	564 608	26.5 18.7	-7.8
Crack cocaine	488 518	22.9 15.9	-7.0
Marijuana	483 818	22.7 25.2	2.5
Heroin	290 252	13.6 7.8	-5.8
All methamphetamines	219 748	10.3 23.0	12.7
Other drugs	85 306	4.0 9.4	5.4
*Total**	2129 3250	100 100	

*Number of missing observations=1.
Sources: ICPSR 9317, FY1996; ICPSR 20120 , FY2006.

The type of drug for which the women were convicted, however, varied among the demographic groups. The primary drugs in which each demographic group was involved are outlined in Tables D1 and D2 (See Appendix D).

In 1996 the majority (50.8 percent) of black women convicted of drug offenses were convicted of offenses that involved crack cocaine. Furthermore, 75.8 percent of all women who were convicted of drug offenses involving crack cocaine were black. The drugs for which white females were most often convicted differed from those for which black women were convicted. Of white women who were convicted of drug offenses, the largest single group (29.9 percent) was involved with marijuana. Convictions for offenses that involved methamphetamines (26.3 percent) were about equally prevalent among white women who were convicted of drug offenses. However, 85.4 percent of all women who were convicted of drug offenses involving methamphetamines were white. The patterns of drug conviction for Hispanic women also differed from those of white or black women. Marijuana (31.2 percent) and cocaine (30.3 percent) were almost equal in their prevalence among Hispanic women, with heroin (26.9 percent) slightly lower. Additionally, 63.8 percent of all women who were convicted of drug offenses that involved heroin were Hispanic.[209]

In 2006, 47 percent of all black women convicted of drug offenses were convicted of offenses that involved crack as the primary drug; this was down by 2.2 percent compared to the 1996 figure. Of all of the women convicted of drug offenses involving crack in 2006, black women were still the majority at 59.1 percent. Once again, the drugs for which white women were convicted in 2006 differed from those of black women. The single largest drug group for white females was methamphetamines (40.1 percent), followed by marijuana (20.2 percent); 72.2 percent of all women who were convicted of methamphetamines as the primary drug, were white (down by 13.2 percent from 1996). For Hispanic women, marijuana continued to be the number one drug at 37.9 percent (up by 6.7 percent), followed once again by powdered cocaine at 26.1 percent (down by 4.2 percent), and methamphetamines at 15.9 percent (up by 11.4 percent). Heroin ranked fourth at 11.7 percent (down by 15.8 percent from 1996). Hispanic women represented 57.9 percent of all women convicted of drug offenses involving heroin and marijuana, followed by 53.8 percent of all women convicted of powdered cocaine offenses.

Comparison of the drugs for which each demographic group was convicted indicate that in 1996 and 2006 the single largest group of women convicted of drug offenses involving crack cocaine was black women. In 1996 the single largest group of women convicted of any drug offense was black women who were sentenced for crimes involving crack cocaine; in 2006, the largest

209   See Table D1, Appendix D.

group was white women convicted of offenses involving methamphetamines, followed by Hispanic women involved with marijuana offenses.

The association between black women and crack cocaine is expected to be important in explaining why black females are represented disproportionately among women who are incarcerated for drug offenses. Given that relatively small amounts of crack cocaine require mandatory minimum sentences, it is predicted that the presence of crack cocaine will prove to have been significant in the decisions to incarcerate, as well as the length of prison sentences, for black females.

The vast majority of women who are convicted of drug offenses in the federal system receive prison sentences. The largest segment of women who received prison terms for drugs in 1996 were those who had been convicted of offenses involving powdered cocaine (484) and crack (435). In 2006 the top categories were marijuana (645) and methamphetamines (689); crack (445) was fourth. Additionally, in 1996, 89.9 percent of women who were convicted of offenses involving crack cocaine were imprisoned, as compared to 86.3 percent of those who were convicted of charges involving powdered cocaine. In 2006, 92.9 percent of the women convicted for offenses involving crack cocaine received a prison sentence (up by 3 percent) as compared to 90.5 percent of those convicted for powder cocaine (up by 4.2 percent). With the exception of the categories "other drugs" and marijuana, the percentage of women within each drug category who received prison sentences exceeded 84 percent in 1996 (Table 6.2). By 2006 all categories except "other drugs," including marijuana, had 86 percent or greater percentages of convicted women receiving prison sentences.

The single largest sentencing category for black women sentenced to prison terms for drug offenses was twelve to thirty-five months in 1996, but by 2006 this had increased to sixty to 119 months. Furthermore, there were differences among the other demographic groups and the two periods of times. In the case of Hispanic women, a sentence of twelve to thirty-five months was most prevalent in both years. White women, in both 1996 and 2006, who were sentenced for drug offenses in federal court most often received no prison sentence or sentences of twelve to thirty-five months. In both 1996 and 2006, the demographic group that was least likely to receive prison sentences was white women.

Based upon the type of drug involved in the offenses, the types of sentences and the length of sentences also varied among the various demographic groups (Tables 6.2, 6.3, and 6.4).

Table 6.2: Mean Prison Sentence (Months) by Type of Drug, 1996 and 2006

Type of drug	Sample		Black Women		White Women		Hispanic Women	
	1996	2006	1996	2006	1996	2006	1996	2006
Powdered cocaine	46.5	63.6	45.0	116.1	37.1	28.4	54.3	52.2
Crack cocaine	59.8	79.8	64.8	102.1	41.2	48.6	49.1	52.3
Heroin	45.0	81.2	44.8	42.2	N/A	26.8	48.7	113.4
Marijuana	21.5	21.3	16.6	31.8	19.0	22.0	25.3	19.6
Methamphetamines	60.4	93.1	N/A	66.2	48.4	83.5	N/A	121.2
Other drugs	43.3	41.3	52.3	30.0	34.0	37.4	43.8	60.3

Source: ICPSR 9317 N=2098 & 20120 N=2983.

Table 6.3: Mean Probation Sentence (months) by Type of Drug, 1996 and 2006

Type of Drug	Sample		Black Women		White Women		Hispanic Women	
	1996	2006	1996	2006	1996	2006	1996	2006
Powdered cocaine	5.4	3.4	5.4	5.1	8.4	6.1	3.4	1.4
Crack cocaine	4.4	2.9	4.1	2.4	5.8	4.2	4.7	1.9
Heroin	6.1	4.7	11.1	4.4	N/A	7.3	3.0	4.0
Marijuana	12.2	5.1	15.6	9.9	14.8	5.6	8.9	4.2
Methamphetamines	6.0	1.8	N/A	6.67	6.0	2.2	N/A	.52
Other drugs	7.2	7.7	6.2	8.40	10.2	9.45	5.2	2.0

Source: ICPSR 9317 N=2098 & 20120 N=2983.

Table 6.4: Mean Sentence of Supervised Release (Months) by Type of Drug and Demographic group, 1996 and 2006

Type of Drug	Sample		Black Women		White Women		Hispanic Women	
	1996	2006	1996	2006	1996	2006	1996	2006
Powdered cocaine	40.8	42.2	41.7	41.2	35.6	34.2	43.3	45.8
Crack cocaine	46.1	47.1	47.0	48.8	40.9	43.3	47.4	50.1
Heroin	41.6	38.2	38.4	37.1	N/A	35.4	44.6	39.5
Marijuana	26.4	31.9	20.00	31.0	24.2	32.1	30.1	32.0
Methamphetamines	46.0	50.5	N/A	48.0	42.3	51.4	N/A	48.1
Other drugs	38.2	32.2	42.2	35.3	32.8	28.3	39.5	42.2

Source: ICPSR 9317, N=2098; Source: ICPSR 20120, N=2978.

Tables 6.2–6.4 report the mean sentences (in months) received by each group of women who were sentenced for drug offenses in 1996 and 2006. Only drugs for which at least one hundred women were convicted are included in the analyses. As indicated, although black females received longer mean prison sentences (64.8 months for crack cocaine) than did other women in 1996, this position was occupied by Hispanic women in 2006, who received an average sentence of 121.2 months for methamphetamines. In 2006, black women convicted for drug offenses involving powdered cocaine were second highest at 116.1 months. Black women convicted of offenses involving crack received a mean prison sentence of 102.1 months—37.3 months (more than three years) longer than in 1996.

In 1996 the greatest difference among the groups arose with drug offenses involving crack cocaine; black women had prison sentences with a mean of 64.8 months, compared to 41 months for white women and 49 months for Hispanic women. In 2006 the disparity in sentencing was experienced by both black and Hispanic women. Black women received significantly longer mean sentences for powdered cocaine (116.1 for black females, 28.4 for white females, 54.3 for Hispanic females) and crack (102.1 for black, 48.6 for white, 52.3 for Hispanic); Hispanic women received much longer mean sentences than the other two groups of women for heroin (113.4 for Hispanic, 42.2 for black, 26.8 for white) as well as for methamphetamines (121.2 for Hispanic, 66.2 for black, and 83.5 for white). It is also important to note that Hispanic women tend to fair badly in all three analyses.

Apparently, there were factors outside of the type of drug that influenced the length of sentences received by black women for crack cocaine offenses. It is expected that the mandatory minimum sentences associated with crack cocaine offenses will provide some explanation for the difference. Because a defendant's criminal history is a legal variable that is normally considered in the sentencing process, it is logical to expect that criminal history or prior record would explain why so many women who were convicted of drug offenses received prison sentences. This does not appear to be supported by the data, however, as the majority of women who were convicted of crimes that involved drugs and who were sentenced to serve time in prison in 1996 and 2006 had little or no prior record.

Approximately 70 percent of the black females, 82 percent of the Hispanic females, and 75 percent of the white females who were convicted of drug offenses in 1996 had minimal or no prior record.[210] In 2006 this pattern continued—60 percent of the black women, 62 percent of the white women, and 82 percent of the Hispanic women—although the percentage of white

---

210   For a full discussion of the final criminal history categories, see the section regarding this variable in chapter three.

and black women with this minimal level of criminal history decreased, the percentage increased for Hispanic women.[211] Considering that the majority of each demographic group falls within category one (which represents one criminal history point or none), one may conclude that the high frequency and long length of incarceration of women convicted of drug offenses was not a result of their prior criminal records in either year.

These findings suggest that the criminal histories or prior records provide little explanation about the prevalence of incarcerative sentences among all demographic groups of women convicted of drug offenses in the federal system during these years. In other words, most of the women who were incarcerated for drug offenses in the federal system did not have criminal histories that would explain why they received prison sentences or why those sentences were so long. Prior research suggests that the mandatory minimum sentencing schemes will provide significant explanation about both the decision to incarcerate and the amount of prison time received for all demographic groups, regardless of the type of drug for which they were convicted. The descriptive analyses of the data appear to substantiate this proposed relationship.

Analyses of the data indicate that black women who were convicted and incarcerated for offenses that involved crack were impacted by the mandatory minimum sentences established by the Anti-Drug Abuse Acts of 1986 and 1988. As shown, approximately 60 percent of the black females in 1996 and 53 percent in 2006 who received prison sentences for drug offenses with mandatory minimum sentences had been convicted of crimes involving crack cocaine. This relationship between black females and convictions for offenses that involved crack cocaine far surpassed any other drug for any demographic group, except in 2006 when 57 percent of white women convicted of drug offenses involving methamphetamines received a prison sentence with a mandatory minimum sentence. Therefore, mandatory minimum sentencing appears to be important in the imprisonment of women convicted of drugs offenses; this was consistent for black women convicted of drug offenses involving crack cocaine in both 1996 and 2006.

Mandatory Minimum Sentences

The war on drugs is defined in this study as the application of the mandatory minimum sentencing provisions contained in the Anti-Drug Abuse Acts of 1986 and 1988, particularly those associated with crack cocaine offenses. The graphs in the previous section indicate that mandatory minimum sentencing is an important factor in the imprisonment of women, particularly black

---

211   ICPSR 9317, FY 1996; ICPSR 20120, FY 2006.

females convicted of crack cocaine offenses. This study examines how the application of the mandatory minimum laws influenced (1) the decision to incarcerate women convicted of drug offenses and (2) the length of prison sentences imposed upon women convicted of drug offenses. It was expected that the mandatory minimum sentences that apply to crack cocaine offenses will provide significant information to explain the disproportionality of black women within the population of women who are incarcerated for drug offenses.

Descriptive analyses of the imposition of mandatory minimum sentencing provide information about the variable itself. The primary questions are:

1. How are the mandatory minimum sentencing provisions applied, that is, which demographic groups are affected most and which types of drugs are most associated with the application of mandatory minimum sentences?

2. Do all women who are convicted of drug offenses with mandatory minimum sentences receive prison sentences?

The mandatory sentences that are applicable to drug cases range from one month to life imprisonment. More than half of the women in the 1996 and 2006 samples of 2,130 and 3,050 women, respectively, convicted of offenses that involved drugs (55.8 percent in 1996 and 54.6 percent in 2006) were convicted of offenses that required mandatory minimum sentences of incarceration. The majority of these women in both years were convicted of drug offenses that required imprisonment for either five years (26.5 percent in 1996 and 22.3 percent in 2006) or ten years (27.3 percent in 1996 and 29.7 percent in 2006).[212] The mean for the 1996 group was 54.4 months, and the median was 60 months; for 2006 the mean increased to 65.6, and the median remained at 60.

The demographics of the women convicted of drug offenses requiring mandatory minimum sentences varied. In 1996 approximately 44.2 percent of the females were convicted of drug offenses that did not require mandatory minimum sentences. Of that group, 27.8 percent were black, 41.2 percent were white, and 31.0 percent were Hispanic. In 2006, approximately the same portion, 45.4 percent of the women, were convicted of drug offenses that did not require mandatory minimum sentences. Of that group, 16.1 percent were black, 41.0 percent Hispanic, and 42.9 percent white. In both years, black women constituted the smallest percentage of the groups that were *not* sentenced for drug offenses that required mandatory minimum sentences; white women constituted the largest group in both years.

---

212 See Tables D.3 and D.4 in Appendix D.

However, of the 55.8 percent who were convicted of drug offenses that required mandatory minimum sentences in 1996, 39 percent were black, 28 percent were white, and 33 percent were Hispanic. In 2006, of the 54.6 percent of the women with drug convictions that required a mandatory minimum sentence, 41 percent were white, 38 percent were Hispanic, and 21.5 percent were black. Although in 1996, black females represented the largest percentage of female drug offenders receiving mandatory minimum sentences, by 2006, white females occupied this unenviable position, followed closely by Hispanic women. Something had changed in the intervening ten years.

Most women convicted of drug offenses that required statutory minimum sentences faced imprisonment of five or ten years. Specifically, in 1996, 28.7 percent of the black, 23.2 percent of the white, and 27.6 percent of the Hispanic women were convicted of drug offenses that required imprisonment of five years; in 2006, 28.4 percent of the black, 23.8 percent of the white, and 17.8 percent of the Hispanic women received a five-year sentence. In comparison, in 1996, 31.6 percent of the black, 28.6 percent of the Hispanic, and 21.8 percent of the white females were convicted of drug offenses with mandatory minimum sentences of ten years; in 2006, the figures stood at 33.9 percent for Hispanic, 29.9 for black, and 25.5 percent for white women.

A within-group comparison of the women who were convicted of drug offenses that required incarceration of five years in 1996 indicates that 37.0 percent were black, 33.6 percent were white, and 29.4 percent were Hispanic. In 2006, 24.3 percent were black, 31.3 percent were Hispanic, and 44.4 percent were white. In other words, 37 percent of the females in 1996 and 24.3 percent of those in 2006, who were convicted of offenses that required imprisonment for five years were black. Although the percentage of black women decreased from 37 percent in 1996 to 24.3 percent in 2006, when one compares this to the fact that black females comprise only approximately 12 percent of the general population, it is evident how disproportionately they were represented among the women who were convicted of drug offenses requiring a five-year prison sentence.

The within-group comparison for offenses that required imprisonment of ten years was: in 1996, 39.5 of the black females, 26.7 percent of the white females, and 33.8 percent of the Hispanic females; and, in 2006, the figures stood at 19.2 percent, 35.8 percent, and 45 percent, respectively. Based upon this analysis, in 1996, black women were convicted of mandatory minimum sentences more often and for longer periods of time than were white or Hispanic women. By 2006, this rate had decreased by almost 20 percent, while the rate for Hispanic women increased by approximately 12 percent and for white women increased by about 10 percent.[213]

It is important to note that not all women convicted of drug offenses that required mandatory minimum sentences of imprisonment were actually sentenced to prison. In 1996, 7.8 percent of the 1,175 women who were convicted for drug offenses requiring mandatory minimum sentences did not receive prison sentences.[214] Of this group, the largest number consisted of those women who were convicted of offenses that required five or ten years of incarceration. In fact, 11.5 percent (64) of the women who were to receive five-year mandatory sentences and 4.2 percent (24) of those who were to receive mandatory minimum sentences of ten years did not actually receive these sentences.

In 2006 only 2 percent (a 5.8 percent decrease from 1996), or thirty-three, of the 1,663 women who were convicted of drug offenses requiring mandatory minimum sentences, did not receive a mandatory minimum sentence. Additionally, a smaller percentage of the women sentenced for an offense with a five-year mandatory minimum sentence attached to it, 3.4 percent (down 8.1 percent from 1996), or twenty-three women, and ten years, 1 percent (down 3.1 percent from 1996), or nine women, did not receive the prescribed mandatory minimum sentence. These statistics indicate a significant reduction in the percentage of women who did not receive a mandatory minimum sentence as compared to women who were similarly situated in 1996.[215]

Of the ninety-two women who were convicted of drug offenses in 1996 that required mandatory minimum sentences of imprisonment but did not receive prison sentences, 35.9 percent were black, 25 percent were Hispanic, and 39.1 percent were white. Of the 460 black females who were convicted of drug offenses requiring mandatory prison terms, 7.2 percent did not receive the mandatory minimum sentence. For Hispanic and white females, the percentages were 5.9 and 11.1, respectively.

In 2006, of the thirty-three women who received a conviction that carried a mandatory minimum sentence but did not receive the required sentence, 39.4 percent were black, 18.2 percent were Hispanic, and 42.45 percent were white. This represented a decrease in the percentage of black and white females and an increase for Hispanic females, as compared to 1996. Of the 357 black females who had mandatory minimums attached to their drug offenses in 2006, 3.6

---

213 What led to these changes? Part of the explanation was the significant increase in the number of white women who were convicted and incarcerated for drug offenses involving methamphetamines.

214 Table D.5, Appendix D.

215 Table D.6, Appendix D.

percent did not receive a prison sentence, and 96.4 percent did. The percentage for Hispanic women was 1 percent, and for white women it was 2.1 percent.

The figures for 2006 indicate that among women who were convicted of drug offenses requiring mandatory minimum sentences, there was an association between demographic group and whether the women actually went to prison.[216] Multivariate analyses will assist in better explicating the association and possible factors affecting the outcome. The results of the multivariate analyses will be discussed in the next chapter.

Although the data indicate that not all women who were convicted of drug offenses requiring mandatory minimum sentences received prison sentences, the only statutorily recognized departure from the mandatory minimum sentences of the 1986 and 1988 Anti-Drug Abuse Acts in 1996 was for substantial assistance. By 2006 there were other legally accepted categories of downward departures, but the ADAAs of 1986 and 1988 remained in effect. The following analyses of the data investigate the role that downward departures played in the sentencing of women convicted of drug offenses requiring mandatory minimum sentences.

Table 6.5: Departures by Demographic Groups with Offenses Requiring Mandatory Minimum Sentences, 1996

Demographic Groups Row pct. Column pct.	Departures				Row totals
	None	*Upward*	*Downward but no reason provided*	*Downward for substantial assistance*	
Black females	228 50.3 39.4	1 .2 50.0	32 7.1 38.1	192 42.4 39.0	**453** **39.2**
Hispanic females	215 56.3 37.2		33 8.6 39.3	134 35.1 27.2	**382** **33.0**
White females	135 42.1 23.4	1 .3 50.0	19 5.9 22.6	166 51.7 33.7	**321** **27.8**
Total Number **Total Row Pct**	**578** **50.0**	**2** **.2**	**84** **7.3**	**492** **42.6**	**1,156** **100.0**

Source: ICPSR 9317, FY1996.

---

216 The chi-square value of 7.16291 at p<.02784 for 1996 and 8.53 at p<.05.

Table 6.6: Departures by Demographic Groups with Offenses Requiring Mandatory Minimum Sentences, 2006

Demographic Groups	Departures						Row Totals
Row pct. Column pct.	*None*	*Upward no reason*	*Upward w/ Booker*	*Downward for substantial assistance*	*Downward no reason*	*Downward w/ Booker*	
Black females	165 46.5 22.9		0 .0 .0	133 37.5 19.2	19 5.4 17.8	38 10.7 31.1	355 21.5
Hispanic females	302 48.4 41.8		1 .2 33.3	215 34.5 31.0	60 9.6 56.1	46 7.4 37.7	624 37.9
White females	255 38.1 35.3		2 .3 66.7	346 51.7 49.9	28 4.2 26.2	38 5.7 31.1	669 40.6
Total Number Total Row Pct	**722** **43.8** 100.0%		**3** **.2** 100.0%	**694** **42.1** 100.0%	**107** **6.5** 100.0%	**122** **7.4** 100.0%	**1648** 100.0%

Source: ICPSR 20120, FY2006.

*The USSC 2006 dataset started reporting information on sentences outside the guidelines range as BOOKERCD, which included departure information after the *U.S. v Booker* decision.

Departures were applied in 50 percent of all cases in 1996 (578) and 43.8 percent of cases (722) in 2006 that involved women convicted of drug offenses requiring mandatory minimum sentencing. In 1996 most of the departures resulted from successful motions for substantial assistance. Black females (39.0 percent) received departures for substantial assistance more often than did Hispanic women (27.2 percent) or white women (33.7 percent). Additionally, in 1996, 51.7 percent of the white females who were convicted of drug offenses that required mandatory minimum sentences benefited from downward departures for substantial assistance, as compared to only 42.4 percent of the black females and 35.1 percent of the Hispanic females (Table 6.5).

In 2006 most of the downward departures were once again for substantial assistance. At that point, white women benefited the most from these departures (49.9 percent) as compared to Hispanic (31 percent) and black (19.2 percent) women. Additionally, in 2006, white women also formed the greatest portion (62 percent) of women who received any type of downward departure as compared to black (54 percent) and Hispanic women (51.5 percent) (Table 6.6).

Downward departures also varied based upon the mandatory minimum sentence that was applied to the drug offense. Most departures were applied to cases in which the mandatory minimum sentences were sixty months (five years) or 120 months (ten years). In 1996, for women convicted of offenses with a mandatory minimum sentence of five years, 38.1 percent received departures for substantial assistance, and 7.0 percent received departures for unknown reasons. In cases that involved mandatory minimum sentences of ten years, 46.9 percent received downward departures for substantial assistance, and 8.1 percent received downward departures for reasons unknown.[217]

By 2006 the types of justifications for downward departures had increased. Of the women sentenced to mandatory minimum sentences for drug offenses, once again, those who were facing sentences of five years (35.8 percent for substantial assistance, 6.4 percent for no given reason, and 8.1 percent under *Booker*) and ten-year sentences (46.6 percent substantial assistance, 7.1 percent for no reason given, and 7.3 percent under Booker) benefited the most from downward departures as compared to women receiving other length sentences.[218]

In comparison, in 1996, 45 percent of the women who received mandatory minimum sentences of five years received downward departures, as compared to 50 percent in 2006. For ten-year sentences, this figure was 55 percent in 1996 and 61 percent in 2006.

The application of downward departures also varied by the type of drug involved. In a comparison of powdered cocaine and crack cocaine, the sentences for cases in 1996 that involved crack (55.3 percent) were more often reduced

217 Table D.7, Appendix D.
218 Table D.8, Appendix D.

by downward departure than sentences for cases involving powdered cocaine (45.9 percent); this was also true in 2006 (56.1 percent of cases for crack and 53 percent for powdered cocaine). Cases in 1996 and 2006 that involved marijuana (51.9 percent and 53.2 percent, respectively), methamphetamines (58.7 percent and 61.2 percent, respectively), and other drugs (46.7 percent and 50 percent, respectively) also received significant downward departures from mandatory minimum sentences (Tables 6.7 and 6.8).

Table 6.7: Departures by Drug Type for Cases with Mandatory Minimum Sentences, 1996

Drugs Row pct. Column pct.	Departures				
	No departure	*Upward departure*	*Downward departure with no reason provided*	*Downward departure for substantial assistance*	**Totals**
Powdered cocaine	194 54.6 33.6	0 .0 .0	31 8.7 36.9	133 37.2 27.0	**358** **31.0**
Crack cocaine	150 44.4 26.0	1 .3 50.0	20 5.9 23.8	167 49.4 33.9	**338** **29.2**
Heroin	106 60.2 18.3	0 .0 .0	16 9.1 19.0	54 30.7 11.0	**176** **15.2**
Marijuana	62 47.3 10.7	1 .8 50.0	7 5.3 8.3	61 46.6 12.4	**131** **11.3**
Methamphetamines	55 41.4 9.5	0 .0 .0	9 6.8 10.7	69 51.9 14.0	**133** **11.5**
Other drugs	11 55.0 1.9	0 .0 .0	1 5.0 1.2	8 40.0 1.6	**20** **1.7**
Column totals	578 50.0	2 .2	84 7.3	492 42.6	**1,156** **100.0**

Source: ICPSR 9317, FY1996.

Table 6.8: Departures by Drug Type for Cases with Mandatory Minimum Sentences, 2006

Drugs Row pct. Column pct.	None	Upward no reason	Upward w/ Booker	Downward substantial assistance	Downward no reason	Downward w/Booker	Total
Powdered cocaine	193 47.0 26.8		0 .0 .0	160 38.9 23.1	30 7.3 28.0	28 6.8 23.0	411 25.0
Crack cocaine	142 44.0 19.7		0 .0 .0	135 41.8 19.5	19 5.9 17.8	27 8.4 22.1	323 19.7
Heroin	61 47.3 8.5		0 .0 .0	47 36.4 6.8	12 9.3 11.2	9 7.0 7.4	129 7.9
Marijuana	79 45.7 11.0		2 1.2 66.7	68 39.3 9.8	13 7.5 12.1	11 6.4 9.0	173 10.5
Methamphetamines	202 38.6 28.1		1 .2 33.3	250 47.8 36.1	27 5.2 25.2	43 8.2 35.2	523 31.8
Other drugs	42 50.0 5.8		0 .0 .0	32 38.1 4.6	6 7.1 5.6	4 4.8 3.3	84 5.1
Column totals	**719** **43.8**		**3** **.2**	**692** **42.1**	**107** **6.5**	**122** **7.4**	**1643** **100.0**

Source: ICPSR 20120, FY2006.

Departures from the provisions of the mandatory minimum sentencing requirements do not necessarily mean that the defendants will not receive a sentence of imprisonment. In 1996 only 7.5 percent of the women who were convicted of drug offenses that required mandatory minimum sentences and who received departures for substantial assistance did not go to prison; in 2006, this figure had dropped to about 2 percent. Therefore, although departures for substantial assistance or other reasons might have been applied to cases that required mandatory minimum sentences, most of the defendants received a sentence of imprisonment (92.2 percent and 98.1 percent in 1996 and 2006, respectively).[219]

The application of downward departure resulted in the reduction of the length of prison sentences but did not keep most of these women from being sentenced to prison. This shall be explored further in the multivariate analyses.

In summary, the descriptive analyses of the imposition of mandatory minimum sentences established that:

1. Within this ten-year period, drug offenses took the lead among the offenses for which women who were convicted of crimes in the federal system were convicted.

2. Considering that black females comprised only about 12 percent of the uninstitutionalized female population, they were represented disproportionately at 34 percent in 1996 (almost three times) and 26.4 percent in 2006 (more than twice as much) among all women convicted in federal court.

3. There was a significant decrease between 1996 and 2006, in the percentage of black women (a drop of 15.4 percent), among women who were convicted of drug offenses in the federal system.

4. The primary drugs for which women were convicted in 1996 were powdered cocaine, crack cocaine, and marijuana. By 2006, the primary drugs were methamphetamines, marijuana, and powdered cocaine.

5. Black women constituted the majority of women who were convicted of drug offenses involving crack cocaine in both 1996 and 2006.

6. In 1996, the single largest group of women convicted of drug crimes was made up of black women sentenced for crack cocaine;

---

219 Tables D.9 and D.10, Appendix D.

in 2006, it was white women convicted of offenses involving methamphetamines, followed by Hispanic women involved with marijuana offenses.

7. The single largest sentencing category for black women sentenced to prison terms for drug offenses was twelve to thirty-five months in 1996, but by 2006 this had increased to sixty to 119 months.

8. Black women convicted of offenses involving crack received a mean prison sentence of 102.1 months, which was 37.3 months (more than three years) longer than in 1996.

9. The majority of women who were convicted of crimes that involved drugs and were sentenced to serve time in prison in both 1996 and 2006 had little or no prior criminal record.

10. Of the black females who received prison sentences for drug offenses with mandatory minimum sentences, approximately 60 percent in 1996 and 53 percent in 2006 were sentenced for offenses involving crack cocaine.

11. In 1996, 28.7 percent of the black, 23.2 percent of the white, and 27.6 percent of the Hispanic women were convicted of drug offenses that required imprisonment of five years; in 2006, 28.4 percent of the black, 23.8 percent of the white, and 17.8 percent of the Hispanic women received five-year sentences. In comparison, in 1996, 31.6 percent of the black, 28.6 percent of the Hispanic, and 21.8 percent of the white females were convicted of drug offenses with mandatory minimum sentences of ten years; in 2006, the percentages were 33.9 for Hispanic, 29.9 for black, and 25.5 for white women.

12. In 1996, black women were convicted of mandatory minimum sentences more often (at a rate of 39.5 percent) and for longer periods of time than were white (26.7 percent) or Hispanic (33.8 percent) women. By 2006, this rate had decreased by almost 20 percent, while for Hispanic women it increased by approximately 12 percent, and for white women increased by about 10 percent.

13. Most of the drug offenses for which women were convicted in 1996 and 2006 had mandatory minimum sentences applied to them.

14. Not all women who were convicted of drug offenses requiring mandatory minimum sentences received prison sentences, but most of them did.

15. The percentage of women with mandatory minimum sentences who did not go to prison varied by demographic group with white women constituting the greatest percentage of those not going to prison.

16. Downward departures were applied to 50 percent of all drug cases that required mandatory minimum sentences in 1996 and 43.8 percent in 2006.

17. The application of downward departures in drug convictions where mandatory minimum sentences would apply varied based upon demographic group (50 percent and 54 percent of cases involving black women, 44 percent and 51.5 percent of Hispanic women's cases, and 58 percent and 62 percent of white women's cases in 1996 and 2006, respectively).

18. The application of downward departures varied based upon type of drug.

    o In 1996, 55.3 percent of the downward departures were for offenses that involved crack cocaine as compared to 45.9 percent for powdered cocaine.

    o In 2006, 56.1 percent of the downward departures were for offenses that involved crack cocaine as compared to 53 percent for powdered cocaine.

19. The vast majority (84.5 percent in 1996 and 98.1 percent in 2006) of the female defendants who had mandatory minimum sentences and received downward departures were sent to prison.

These findings demonstrate that mandatory minimum sentencing has played a significant part in the war on drugs. Most women who were convicted of drug offenses had mandatory minimum sentences applied to their offenses and received prison sentences. Although there have been additional legally accepted reasons for the application of downward departures, and the percentage of women receiving them has increased, the application of downward departures has not tended to negate a sentence of imprisonment.

In chapter seven the investigation of mandatory minimum sentences and downward departures and their influence on: (1) the decision to impose mandatory minimum sentences in cases where mandatory minimum sentences were applicable and (2) the length of prison term imposed in cases that required imposition of mandatory minimum sentences, will continue with the multivariate analyses of the variables. Now we will focus on an analysis specific to black females and crack cocaine.

Black Women with Convictions for Crack Cocaine

In 1996 black females (370 individuals) formed the single largest group of female drug offenders involved with crack cocaine as the primary substance underlying their drug convictions. (Forty-four were Hispanic, and seventy-four were white.[220]) This was also the case in 2006 (276 were black, 45 were Hispanic, and 158 were white).[221] Moreover, 75.8 percent of the black females who were convicted of drug offenses in 1996 were convicted of offenses that involved crack cocaine; in 2006, this figure was 57.6 percent. Although the percentage decreased, black females continued to be represented disproportionately among women who were convicted of drug offenses and among women who were convicted of drug offenses involving crack cocaine.

It is the high prevalence of convictions of black women for drug offenses involving crack cocaine that is expected to provide significant explanation for the disproportionate representation of black women among female drug offenders in the federal prison system. In 1996 and 2006, respectively, 89.9 percent and 92.9 percent of the women who were convicted of drug offenses involving crack cocaine received prison sentences. What were the factors that influenced the decision to incarcerate or impose certain sentence lengths on these women? Was it the mandatory minimum sentences applied to their offenses, their prior records, and/or the amount of crack cocaine involved? The following descriptive analyses provide some insight into these questions.

Of the black women who received prison terms for drug offenses that involved crack cocaine and carried mandatory minimum sentences, the most prevalent sentences in both 1996 (34 percent) and 2006 (38 percent), were sentences of sixty to 119 months. In comparison, approximately 54 percent of the black females who were sentenced to prison for offenses that involved crack cocaine but did not carry mandatory minimum sentences received twelve to thirty-five months (from one year to just under three years) in 1996. Although this was also the sentence range most prevalent for their counterparts in 2006 (36 percent), there was a significant increase in the percentage of black females who received sentences of thirty-six to fifty-nine months (30 percent)

---

220   Chi-square 490.69040, significance p<.00001.
221   Chi-square 5.352, significance p<.0001.

and sixty to 119 months (26 percent), as compared to 1996 (19 percent and 6 percent, respectively).

It appears that applying mandatory minimum sentences to offenses that involve crack cocaine may impact the length of prison sentences received by black females. However this analysis does not control for or take into account prior record, amount of drugs involved, or other legal sentencing factors. This control will be included in the analyses in the next chapter.

Although female drug offenders, including black women, tended to have minimal or no prior criminal record, it is logical to question whether the black women convicted of drug offenses involving crack cocaine who received prison sentences with mandatory minimums, had prior records that might have affected the decisions to incarcerate them and the length of the sentences they received. However, this does not appear to be the case. More than 60 percent of the imprisoned black females who were convicted of drug offenses that involved crack cocaine and required mandatory minimum sentencing in 1996 had little or no criminal history. By 2006, the percentage had decreased to 48 percent although the categories of little or no prior record continued to be the most prevalent single category among black women sentenced to prison with mandatory minimum sentences for offenses involving crack cocaine.

Specifically, 60 percent of the women in 1996 had zero to one points for prior criminal history; 15 percent were in category two and therefore had two or three points; 10 percent were in category three with four to six points; and fewer than 5 percent were in categories four through six with more than six points (Figure 6.12). In 2006, the percentage had changed to 48 percent for category one (-12 percent), 14 percent in category two (-1 percent), 20 percent in category three (+10 percent), 11 percent in category four, 4 percent in category five, and 3 percent in category six. It does not appear that the criminal histories of the women was a significant factor in the decision to incarcerate black females for offenses involving crack cocaine when mandatory minimum sentences were applicable in 1996. It is possible that it was more of a factor in 2006, and the multivariate analysis should provide additional information regarding the effect of mandatory minimums on sentencing of black women for drug offenses involving crack cocaine.

Because of the relationship between relatively small amounts of crack cocaine and mandatory minimum sentencing, an important inquiry is: what is the relationship between varying amounts of crack cocaine, mandatory minimum sentences, and the imprisonment of black females? The majority of cases involved black women who received prison sentences for drug offenses in which the primary drug was crack cocaine in amounts of less than five hundred grams (70 percent in 1996 and 68 percent in 2006). Most of the black women (75 percent in 1996 and 73 percent in 2006) who were sentenced to prison for offenses that involved crack cocaine were sentenced under mandatory minimum sentencing schemes.

This provides some indication of how the mandatory minimum sentences applied to crack cocaine offenses impacted black females in the federal system. If these women had been convicted of offenses involving powdered cocaine, a more concentrated form of cocaine than crack cocaine, the mandatory minimum threshold of five hundred grams would not have been met, and it is doubtful that they would have received prison sentences.

Analyses of the federal sentencing data for 1996 and 2006 indicate that most of the black females who were convicted of crack cocaine offenses received sentences of ten years, although most drug amounts were five hundred grams or less. The majority of black women who were sentenced to prison for drug offenses that involved crack cocaine (58 percent in 1996 and 76 percent in 2006) were usually convicted of crimes involving less than five hundred grams of the drug.

In summary, the descriptive analyses of the data indicate:

1. The majority of women who were sentenced for drug offenses that involved crack cocaine in 1996 and 2006 were black.

2. Approximately half of the black females who were sentenced for drug offenses were sentenced for crimes that involved crack cocaine (in 1996, 50.8 percent and in 2006, 47.5 percent).

3. Because of the association of black females with crack cocaine (approximately half of the black females were convicted for offenses that involved crack cocaine), the mandatory minimum sentencing schemes applied to crack cocaine offenses appear to be a major factor in explaining the overrepresentation of black females among females incarcerated for drug offenses.

4. Because of the association of black females with crack cocaine, the mandatory minimum sentencing schemes applied to offenses that involved crack cocaine may explain the length of prison sentences that black females received.

5. But for the low threshold (as compared to powdered cocaine and marijuana) that triggered mandatory minimum sentencing, the amount of drugs does not seem to explain the type of sentence or amount of time received by black females convicted of drug offenses involving crack cocaine.

Although these analyses provide very important information about what happened, that is, the relationship between the war on drugs and the incarceration of black females, these descriptive analyses are inadequate to develop further conclusions. Questions regarding the significance of alternative explanations of the disproportionality, such as differences in offending behavior, or prior records, remain after performance of the descriptive analyses. In chapter seven the results of several multivariate analyses will be discussed to determine which factors, including prior record and amount of drugs, may explain the severe sentences received by black females convicted of crack cocaine offenses. Based upon the descriptive analyses, it is predicted that the statutory requirements establishing the mandatory minimum sentencing applied to crack cocaine offenses will be significant predictors regarding the incarceration of black females for both 1996 and 2006. The multivariate analyses discussed in chapter seven inform us about the influences of these variables on whether women in general, and black females specifically, who are convicted of drug offenses, particularly those that involved crack cocaine, received a prison sentence, and if so, the length of prison sentence received. These analyses will assist us in answering an important policy question: what effect does mandatory minimum sentencing for small amounts of crack cocaine have on the incarceration of black women convicted of crack offenses?

CHAPTER SEVEN

Investigating Why It Happened: Multivariate Analyses of the Data

Vanessa W. – Twenty-Three Years, Four Months for Conspiracy to Possess with Intent to Distribute Cocaine Base[222]

Vanessa grew up in a small community in Florida. She was raised in a strict and religious environment. When Vanessa was nineteen, her mother committed suicide, and she became the provider and caretaker for her fourteen-year-old brother and eleven-year-old sister, all while feeling devastated inside. Vanessa discontinued her education and worked in order to provide for her siblings. Several months after her mother's death, Vanessa met a man named Ron. He was ten years older than her; he helped guide her and her siblings, and he seemed to care for them all. Vanessa initially thought he was a successful businessman only to find out later that he was a drug dealer. Vanessa eventually wanted to move away from Ron and the life he led. She asked his permission to do so, but it was too late.

At age twenty-one, Vanessa was convicted of conspiracy to possess with the intent to distribute cocaine base. Because she feared Ron, she did not provide the federal investigators with any information against him. Because of her fear-induced silence, Vanessa received a sentence of twenty-three years and four months, while Ron remained free. While Vanessa was serving her time, her brother was murdered—just a week before he was accepted into college. The perpetrator of the homicide received a two-year sentence.

222   http://november.org/thewall/cases/wade-v/wade-v.html. 11/27/2009.

Sentence: twenty-three years, four months for conspiracy to possess
with intent to distribute cocaine base

Although the descriptive analyses in chapter six provide important information
about key variables, important questions remain about the impact of these
variables and their effect on: (1) the imposition of mandatory minimum
sentences of five or ten years, (2) if prison sentences are ordered, and (3)
the length of prison sentences imposed on black women convicted of crack
cocaine offenses. The multivariate analyses allowed for the testing of several
factors or variables that may have affected the disproportional representation
of black women among females incarcerated for drug offenses within the
federal prison system. Although the descriptive analyses indicated that prior
record and drug amount were not significant in explaining the relationship
between crack offenses and the decision and length of incarceration of women,
particularly black women, the multivariate analyses enable us to determine if
their effects were statistically significant. There is also the issue of how crack
cocaine was punished as compared to powdered cocaine. Questions regarding
the impact of the inherent disparity of the 100:1 ratio of powdered to crack
cocaine on black women convicted of drug offenses will also be considered
in this chapter.

The findings for each research question were as follows:

Research Question One

*Did being convicted of a drug offense involving crack cocaine increase the
odds that a mandatory minimum sentence of five or ten years would be imposed
in cases that involved: (a) all women in general and (b) black females specifically?
How did the two years compare to each other?*

The sample used to answer this question consisted of *all women* who
were convicted of drug offenses that had statutory mandatory minimum
imprisonment requirements. There was also an analysis based upon a sample
of all women who were convicted of offenses involving crack or powdered
cocaine and for which mandatory minimum prison sentences were applicable
in each of the two years (1996 and 2006, separately).

The primary inquiries for question one are whether crack cocaine is
significant in predicting if (a) all women and (b) black women received
mandatory sentences of five or ten years. The findings were as follows:

Crack cocaine was statistically significant in 1996. Women who were
convicted of drug offenses that involved crack cocaine and that required
mandatory minimum sentences were twice as likely (2.06 times) to receive

five-year mandatory minimum sentences than if the offenses involved other types of drug. In other words, in 1996, women who were convicted of drug offenses involving drugs other than crack cocaine were less likely to receive five-year mandatory minimums than women who were convicted of offenses that involved crack cocaine.[223]

In 2006, crack cocaine was not statistically significant. It therefore appears that, based upon the sample of all women who were sentenced in 2006 for drug offenses, crack cocaine provided less of an explanation of why these women received sentences of five years.[224]

To investigate the relationship between demographic group membership and the effect of substantively relevant variables on the imposition of five-year mandatory minimum sentences, the sample was divided by demographic group, and the model was tested separately against the subsamples.

Crack cocaine was a significant predictor in whether black and Hispanic women received five-year mandatory minimum sentences in 1996 but not in 2006. Based upon these analyses, black women who were convicted of crack cocaine offenses were twice as likely to receive mandatory minimum sentences of five years in 1996 than if they were sentenced for offenses that involved other drugs. However, this was not a significant factor in 2006 and therefore did not explain why they received five-year sentences.

Crack cocaine was also significant in predicting the odds of a mandatory minimum sentence of five years for a Hispanic woman convicted of a drug offense in 1996 but not in 2006. In 1996, Hispanic women were more than three times (3.3:1) as likely to receive mandatory minimum sentences of five years if sentenced for drug offenses involving crack cocaine than if another drug was involved.

Crack cocaine was not statistically significant in predicting the odds that white females would receive mandatory minimum sentences of five years in 1996 or 2006; neither was downward departure.

Therefore, it is clear that in 1996, crack cocaine was a factor in the application of five-year mandatory minimum sentences for black and Hispanic females but not white females; it was not a factor in 2006 for any of the groups.

The next inquiry involves determining the effects of these variables on the imposition of ten-year sentences. As expected from the descriptive analyses, crack cocaine was a significant factor that influenced the odds that a woman

---

223 The interaction term of demographic group with crack cocaine was originally tested but found to be highly correlated with demographic group. The interaction term was deleted from this analysis in order to determine the effect of demographic group membership on the dependent variable.

224 In 2006 the application of a downward departure was significant at p<.0001 and indicated a woman less likely (.60) to receive a five-year sentence if applied to her case.

convicted of a drug offense involving crack cocaine, as compared to another type of drug, would receive a mandatory minimum sentence of ten years in both years. In 1996, however, the effect was negative (.50: 1). Women convicted of crack cocaine offenses were almost half as likely to receive ten-year prison sentences than if the offenses involved drugs other than crack cocaine. In 2006, the effect was positive: women convicted of drug offenses that involved crack were five times more likely to receive ten-year mandatory minimum sentences than if the offenses involved other drugs.

To better understand the effect of crack cocaine on the imposition of mandatory minimum sentences of ten years for each racial/ethnic group, the sample was divided by demographic group and the model analyzed separately for each group.

Crack cocaine was significant in both years in predicting if black females received mandatory minimum sentences of ten years. The effect of crack as the drug involved, as compared to other types of drugs, on the odds that a black female received this sentence was 0.49:1 in 1996 and 75:1 in 2006. In other words, black women convicted of drug offenses involving crack cocaine were less likely to receive mandatory minimum sentence of ten years in 1996 but were very likely to receive ten-year sentences in 2006.

Crack cocaine was also significant in predicting whether Hispanic females received mandatory minimum sentences of ten years in 1996 and 2006. If a Hispanic female was convicted of a drug offense involving crack cocaine in 1996, she was one-third as likely (.31:1) to receive a mandatory sentence of ten years than if another drug was involved; in 2006 she was almost three times more likely to receive the ten-year sentence.

Crack cocaine was not statistically significant for white females in 1996, but it was in 2006. White women convicted of drug offenses involving crack were 2.6 times more likely to receive ten-year prison sentences in 2006 than if others drugs were involved.

In summary, in 1996, there was a greater probability that black females convicted of drug offenses involving crack cocaine, as compared to other types of drugs, would receive five-year mandatory minimum sentences. In 2006, the five-year sentence was not significant, but the ten-year sentence was; black women were seventy-five times more likely to receive ten-year sentences than if other drugs were involved. Thus, in 2006, the odds greatly increased for the imposition of ten-year sentences for black females convicted of drug offenses involving crack cocaine.

Research Question Two

Did being convicted of drug offenses involving crack cocaine increase the likelihood of incarceration for all women? How did the two years compare to each other?

The sample consisted of all women convicted of drug offenses.

Crack cocaine was significant in both 1996 and 2006. In 1996, being convicted of a drug offense involving crack cocaine, as compared to other drugs, decreased the odds of a woman receiving a prison sentence to 0.54:1; in 2006 it increased the odds to 1.5:1. In other words, in 1996, women who were convicted of crack cocaine offenses were half as likely to receive prison sentences than if other drugs were involved. By 2006 a crack cocaine offense made women more than 1.5 times more likely to receive prison sentences.

Research Question Three

Did being convicted of drug offenses involving crack cocaine increase the length of prison sentences for all women? How did the two years compare to each other?

The sample consisted of all women convicted of drug offenses. The findings indicate that crack cocaine did have a statistically significant effect on the length of sentences received by women who were incarcerated for drugs in both 1996 and 2006. Women who were convicted of drug offenses involving crack cocaine tended to receive prison sentences that were 29 percent longer in 1996 and 37 percent longer in 2006 than women who were convicted of offenses involving other types of drugs.

Research Question Four

Did being convicted of drug offenses involving crack cocaine increase the length of prison sentences for black females? How did the two years compare to each other?

This question involves testing the effect of crack cocaine on the length of prison sentences received by black females. Among women who were convicted of drug offenses and who received prison sentences in 1996, crack cocaine had a statistically significant effect on the length of prison sentences received by black women, but not by Hispanic or white females. Black females who were convicted of drug offenses involving crack cocaine received sentences that were 49 percent longer than if other drugs were involved.

In 2006, crack cocaine was also statistically significant in predicting the total length of prison sentences received by black females, but not Hispanic or white females. In 2006, black females convicted of drug offenses involving crack cocaine received sentences that were almost twice as long as if other drugs were involved.[225]

In summary: Conviction of drug offenses that involved crack cocaine increased the length of prison sentences received by black females (49 percent in 1996 and 99.8 percent in 2006).

Research Question Five

Did mandatory minimum sentencing increase the amount of prison time received by black females who were convicted of crack cocaine offenses? What impact, if any, did their prior records, amount of drugs involved in the offense, role adjustments, or the application of downward departure have on these sentences? How did the two years compare to each other?

While question one tested the effect of crack on the imposition of mandatory minimum sentences, this research question examines the effect that mandatory minimum sentencing had on the length of prison sentences received by black females convicted of crack cocaine offenses.

Mandatory minimum sentencing for drugs was significant in both years for black females. If a mandatory minimum sentence was applicable in a case involving a black female convicted of a drug offense in which crack cocaine was the primary drug, the prison sentence was 83.6 percent longer in 1996 and 98 percent longer in 2006 than similar cases in which no mandatory minimum sentence for drugs was involved.

The prior records of the women were significant in both years; the greater the record, the longer the sentence (588 percent in 1996 and 36 percent longer in 2006).

Although the amount of drugs was not a significant factor in the length of sentence a black woman convicted of a crack cocaine offense received in 1996, it was in 2006; an increase in the amount of drugs increased the length of sentence received.

In 1996 and 2006, the application of downward departures was statistically significant. If a downward departure was applied in a case that involved a black female convicted of a crack cocaine offense, the sentence tended to be 61 percent shorter in 1996 and 62 percent shorter in 2006 than if no downward departure was applied.

Additionally, if a judge applied a role adjustment to the sentence, the effect was a 21.8 percent and 29 percent shorter sentence in 1996 and 2006, respectively.

---

225 Mandatory minimum sentencing was significant for all three groups for both years. This finding indicates the need to investigate the relationship between incarceration and drugs other than crack cocaine for Hispanic and white females.

Question five can be answered as follows: for both 1996 and 2006, mandatory minimum sentencing increased the amount of prison time received by black females who were convicted of drug offenses involving crack cocaine. The effect in 2006 was greater. Downward departures decreased the length of prison sentences in both years with approximately the same effect. The prior record of black women convicted of crack cocaine offenses increased their prison sentences in both years. The amount of drugs involved was not a factor in the length of sentences received by black women convicted of crack offenses in 1996, but it was in 2006; the greater the amount of drugs, the longer the prison sentence. An important factor that mitigated the length of sentences received by black women convicted of drug offenses involving crack cocaine was role adjustments. When judges applied role adjustments, the prison sentences received by black women convicted of crack offenses tended to be shorter in both years.

Research Question Six

Did mandatory minimum sentencing increase the likelihood that women who were sentenced for crack cocaine offenses would receive prison sentences? What impact, if any, did the application of downward departure have on these sentences? How did the two years compare to each other?

In this analysis, the samples consisted of all women convicted of crack cocaine offenses.

Mandatory minimum sentencing was significant in 1996, but not 2006, in predicting if women who were convicted of drug offenses that involved crack cocaine received prison sentences. In 1996, such women were 7.4 times more likely to receive prison sentences than if no mandatory minimum were applicable to their cases.

Downward departure was significant in both years and lessened the likelihood of a woman receiving a prison sentence if convicted of a drug offense involving crack cocaine (.13 percent in 1997 and 0.09 percent in 2006).

Research Question Seven

Did mandatory minimum sentencing increase the likelihood that women who were convicted of drug offenses involving drugs other than crack cocaine would receive prison sentences? What impact, if any, did the application of downward departure have on the sentences? How did the two years compare to each other?

The sample included only those women who were convicted of drug offenses in which drugs other than crack cocaine were involved.

Mandatory minimum sentencing was significant in both years. The odds were 3.62:1 in 1996 and 4.64:1 in 2006 that a woman would receive a prison sentence if she was convicted of a drug offense that involved a drug other than crack cocaine and for which there was a statutory minimum sentence. However, the influence of mandatory minimum sentencing was much less in this analysis than in the analysis of offenses that involved crack in 1996 where the odds were 7.4:1.

The application of downward departures was significant in both years. When applied in 1996, the odds were lessened to 0.18:1 (and to 0.13:1 in 2006) that a woman would receive a prison sentence if she was convicted of an offense for a drug other than crack cocaine and for which there was an applicable mandatory minimum.

Question seven can be answered as follows: mandatory minimum sentencing increased the odds that a woman who was convicted of a drug offense other than crack cocaine received a prison sentence. The application of a downward departure slightly decreased the odds of imprisonment for women convicted of drug offenses involving drugs other than crack cocaine when the offense carried with it a mandatory minimum; the effect was similar in both years.

Research Question Eight

Did mandatory minimum sentencing increase the likelihood of receiving prison sentences among black females who were sentenced for drug offenses in which crack cocaine was the primary drug? What impact, if any, did the application of downward departure have on the sentence? What impact, if any, did the prior records of the women or the amount of drugs involved have on the likelihood that the women would receive prison sentences? How did the two years compare to each other?

The sample used to investigate this question consisted of black females who were convicted of drug offenses involving crack cocaine.

Mandatory minimum sentencing had a statistically significant effect in 1996 but not in 2006 on the odds that black females convicted of drug offenses involving crack cocaine would receive prison sentences. The odds were 5:1 in 1996 that these women would receive prison sentences. Downward departure was significant in both years: the odds that black women who were convicted of drug offenses involving crack cocaine would receive prison sentences were decreased in 1996 by 0.10:1 and in 2006 by 0.13:1 when downward departure was applied. The prior record of the women was a significant factor in both years. In 1996 the prior record increased the odds by 1.76:1, and in 2006 by 2:1, that black women convicted of drug offense involving crack cocaine would receive prison sentences. The amount of drugs involved was not a significant factor in 1996, but it was in 2006 (1.45:1) in increasing the likelihood that these women would receive prison sentences.

Question eight can be answered as follows: in 1996 mandatory minimum sentencing increased the odds that black females convicted of drug offenses that involved crack cocaine would receive prison sentences; by 2006 mandatory minimum sentencing did not have an effect on her likelihood of incarceration. Downward departure decreased the odds that black women convicted of drug offenses involving crack cocaine would receive prison sentences in both 1996 and 2006, and the effect was basically the same in both years. The women's prior records were more of a factor in 2006 than 1996, and although the amount of drugs involved in the offenses was not a significant factor in the odds of their incarceration in 1996, it was in 2006.

Research Question Nine

Did being convicted of a drug offense involving crack cocaine as compared to powder cocaine increase the likelihood that a woman would receive (a) a five-year or (b) a ten-year sentence? How did the two years compare to each other?

This analysis included a sample of women who were convicted of drug offenses involving crack or powdered cocaine. Crack cocaine was significant in 1996 but not in 2006 in predicting the imposition of five-year sentences; women who were convicted of offenses that involved crack cocaine and who received mandatory minimum sentences were less likely in 1996 (.28:1) to receive sentences of five years than if the offenses involved powdered cocaine.

Crack cocaine was significant in the imposition of ten-year sentences in both years. In 1996, women convicted of offenses that involved crack were 3.4 times more likely to receive sentences of ten years than if powdered cocaine was involved; by 2006 the likelihood increased to more than twenty-eight times.[226]

In summary, the imposition of a five-year prison sentence was much less likely in both years if the drug was crack cocaine as compared to powdered cocaine. A conviction for crack cocaine as opposed to powdered cocaine greatly increased the odds of a ten-year prison sentence in both years, with a major increase in the odds in 2006.

---

226 When crack cocaine is compared to other drugs, the odds are 1.68:1.

Summary

The following summarizes the primary findings of the multivariate analyses:

1. In 1996 there was a greater probability that black females convicted of drug offenses involving crack cocaine would receive five-year mandatory minimum sentences than black females convicted of drug offenses involving drugs other than crack cocaine. In 2006 this changed, and black females convicted of drug offenses involving crack cocaine were much more likely to receive ten-year sentences than if other types of drugs were involved. (RQ1)

2. In 1996, among all women who were convicted of drug offenses, being convicted of drug offenses involving crack cocaine as compared to other drugs decreased the odds of a woman receiving a prison sentence to 0.54:1; in 2006 it increased the odds to 1.5:1. (RQ2)

3. Among women who were convicted of drug offenses, women who were convicted of drug offenses involving crack cocaine tended to receive prison sentences that were 29 percent longer in 1996 and 37 percent longer in 2006, than women who were convicted of offenses involving other types of drugs. (RQ3)

4. Among black women who were convicted of drug offenses, conviction of drug offenses involving crack cocaine increased the length of prison sentences received by black females (49 percent in 1996 and 99.8 percent in 2006), than if other types of drugs were involved. (RQ4)

5. In both 1996 and 2006, mandatory minimum sentencing increased the amount of prison time received by black females who were convicted of drug offenses that involved crack cocaine; (83.6 percent longer in 1996 and 98 percent longer in 2006). (RQ5)

6. Downward departures decreased the length of prison sentences in both years with approximately the same effect (61 percent and 62 percent) for black women sentenced for drug offenses involving crack cocaine. (RQ5)

7. Prior record was a significant factor in the length of prison sentences received by black women convicted of drug offenses involving crack cocaine in both 1996 and 2006; the sentences

were 588 percent longer in 1996 and 36 percent longer in 2006. (RQ5)

8. The application of role adjustments shortened the prison sentences received by black women convicted of drug offenses involving crack cocaine in 1996 (21.8 percent shorter) and in 2006 (29 percent shorter). (RQ5)

9. Mandatory minimum sentencing was significant in 1996, but not 2006, in predicting if women who were convicted of drug offenses involving crack cocaine received prison sentences. In 1996, such women were 7.4 times more likely to receive prison sentences than if no mandatory minimums were applicable to their cases. (RQ6)

10. Downward departure was significant in both years and lessened the likelihood of a women receiving a prison sentence if convicted of a drug offense involving crack cocaine (.13 percent in 1997 and 0.09 percent in 2006). (RQ6)

11. Mandatory minimum sentencing increased the odds that a woman who was convicted of a drug offense for a drug other than crack cocaine received a prison sentence; (3.62:1 in 1996 and 4.64:1 in 2006.) (RQ7)

12. The application of a downward departure slightly decreased the odds of imprisonment for women convicted of drug offenses involving drugs other than crack cocaine when the offenses carried with them mandatory minimums, and the effect was similar in both years; (0.18:1 in 1996 and 0.13:1 in 2006). (RQ7)

13. In 1996 mandatory minimum sentencing increased the odds that black females convicted of drug offenses that involved crack cocaine would receive prison sentences (5:1); however, by 2006, mandatory minimum sentencing did not have an effect on the likelihood of incarceration for these women. (RQ8)

14. Downward departure decreased the odds that black women convicted of drug offenses involving crack cocaine would receive prison sentences in both 1996 and 2006, and the effect was basically the same in both years: 0.10:1 in 1996 and 0.13:1 in 2006. (RQ8)

15. In 1996, mandatory minimum sentences had the greatest influence on the odds of black women who were convicted of

crack cocaine offenses receiving prison sentences (5:1), but in 2006 their prior records had the greatest influence (2:1). (RQ8)

16. The imposition of a five-year prison sentence was much less likely in both years if the drug was crack cocaine as compared to powdered cocaine. A conviction for crack cocaine as opposed to powdered cocaine greatly increased the odds of a ten-year prison sentence in both years, with a major increase in the odds in 2006. (RQ9)

Overall, we see that the impact of the war on drugs on the incarceration of black women has changed in the last ten years. A conviction for crack cocaine increased the likelihood of incarceration for black women in 1996 (83.6 percent) and even more in 2006 (98 percent). Furthermore, crack cocaine increased the length of prison sentences for black women by 49 percent in 1996 and 99.8 percent in 2006. Black women with crack convictions were more likely to receive five-year sentences in 1996 and ten-year sentences in 2006. The prior criminal records of these black females were significant in both years, and the amounts of drugs involved were significant in 2006 in explaining their incarceration.

These findings, along with those from the descriptive analyses, have important implications for public policy. They substantiate that the federal drug laws for small amounts of crack cocaine had a significant impact on both the likelihood of incarceration of black women as well as the length of sentences they received. The drug laws regarding crack cocaine have brought black women into prison at a disproportionate rate. The decisions to send them to prison and the long sentences they received were related more to mandatory minimums for small amounts of drugs than their involvement in large amounts of drugs or their prior records.

CHAPTER EIGHT

(Un)Intended Victims?: Politics, Power, and the Status of Black Women

---

Hasan A.H. – Life in Prison for Crack Conspiracy[227]

Hasan was twenty-five years old, the mother of two young daughters, and six months pregnant when she began to serve two natural life sentences, two forty-year sentences, two twenty-year sentences, plus five- and four-year sentences for crack conspiracy. She had no prior criminal record, was charged with a nonviolent offense, and was not arrested for possession, purchase, and/or sale of any drugs, although those are the charges for which she was ultimately convicted.

Hasan states that she was prosecuted for these offenses because she refused to perjure herself and testify against a family member. She was offered a deal in which all of the charges would be dropped against her if she testified. She refused. The man who was arrested in possession of the drugs received a nonprosecution agreement. In exchange for his cooperation, he did not receive the mandatory sentence (probation to five years imprisonment) applicable to his conviction. However, Hasan and the other codefendants received life, life, and ten years based upon the government's assertion that the powder cocaine that was the subject of the case was to be converted to crack. Hasan indicates that she was also convicted of drug offenses that other government witnesses were charged with; they faced imprisonment but instead received immunity, leniency, or reduced sentences because of their cooperation and testimony against others.

Sentence: life in prison for crack conspiracy

---

227   http://november.org/thewall/cases/hasan-h/hasan-h.html. 11/27/2009.

Without a doubt, black women have been severely impacted by the drug laws that place people in prison for small amounts of crack cocaine or crack cocaine conspiracy. They are also often harmed by substantial assistance, as in most instances, they are not able to provide the information the government wants in exchange for leniency because of their low status in the drug market relative to the men with whom they are involved. Instead, it is the men who controlled the drug deals, directed the women, and were directly involved with the drugs, who use substantial assistance against the women in order to secure reduced sentences for themselves. These situations have been repeated for decades. Black women have been serving extraordinary sentences for playing no or relatively small roles in drug deals. They are often snared into the system because of their association with the drug dealer and not because of the magnitude of their own actions. Even if punishment is appropriate, the lengths of some of their sentences are not justified. How could this happen in the first place? And why have black woman in these situations been allowed to be targeted for so long?

As a former legislator, I understand the reluctance of many people to involve themselves in legislative processes, but I am also keenly aware of the need for citizens to do so. To better understand the impact of policies, both their enactment and implementation, one should be familiar with the political context that surrounded their development. In this chapter I will discuss how two sociological perspectives and theories of public policy development may help to explain the political context surrounding the enactment of the Anti-Drug Abuse Acts of 1986 and 1988. This may also provide some answer to the question: *how could this happen?*

Theories of the Public Policy Process

Conflict theories explain crime and justice by focusing attention on the struggles among individuals and/or groups among whom power differentials exist.[228] These theories provide a key to understanding both the politics of law and order and the character of the criminal justice process. The theories concentrate on the divisions within society and the ultimate struggle over scarce resources. The divisions within society produce conflict over two areas: (1) available benefits (i.e., *interests*) such as status, power, and material well-being; and (2) *values*—norms and moral differences that exist in society.[229] There are various conflict theories. The first application of conflict theory

---

228 Robert J. Lilly, Francis T. Cullen, and Richard A. Ball. *Criminological Theory: Context and Consequences.* (Thousand Oaks, CA: Sage, 1995), 132–133.

229 Stuart A. Scheingold. *The Politics of Law and Order: Street Crime and Public Policy.* (New York, NY: Longman, 1984), 224.

to criminology was made by George Vold in the 1950s.[230] He posited that humans join together in groups in order to work collectively to meet their needs. When a group no longer meets the needs of its members, it is disbanded, and new groups are formed. In the attempt to have their needs met, groups often have conflicts with other groups with similar personal interests. Vold argued that the legislative process and crime control directly reflect conflict between interest groups that all want the laws to reflect their interests and provide them with police power.[231]

Another sociologist, Ralf Darendorf, also applied the conflict theory to criminology but in a manner somewhat different from Vold. Darendorf proposed that society does not operate on a consensus model but rather that people are forced to constrain themselves. This forced constraint is what binds them together. Darendorf argued that society includes the powerful and the powerless, all comprising interest groups. When the interests of the groups clash—which, he argues, happens constantly—social change occurs.[232]

Austin Turk expanded the conflict approach.[233,234] He argued, "Criminality is not a biological, psychological, or even behavioral phenomenon, but a social status defined by the way in which an individual is perceived, evaluated, and treated by legal authorities."[235] Turk posited that decision makers define criminal status.

Based upon both my academic research and my experience as a legislator, I find William Chambliss's conflict theory of law, order, and power to provide a critical perspective for understanding how legislation such as the Anti-Drug Abuse Acts of 1986 and 1988, with the associated 100:1 differential for powdered and crack cocaine, could be enacted and implemented. Chambliss's perspective evolved from those of Vold, Darendorf, and Turk, and focuses more on the role of political influence in the enactment and enforcement of laws.

Law, Order, and Power

The study of crime and laws should not focus upon "laws in the books,"

---

230 George Vold. *Theoretical Criminology*. (New York, NY: Oxford University Press, 1958).
231 Vold, 1958.
232 Ralf Darendorf. *Class and Class Conflict in Industrial Society*. (Stanford, CA: Stanford University Press, 1959).
233 Austin Turk. *Criminality and Legal Order*. (Chicago, IL: Rand McNally, 1969).
234 ----. *Political Criminality: The Defiance and Defense of Authority*. (Beverly Hills, CA: Sage. 1982).
235 Turk, 1969.

but rather "law in action."[236] Law in action includes the enactment and implementation of laws, as well as the adjudication and the application of sanctions for breaking the law. The laws that define deviancy and illegality result from political activity. Deviancy is not a moral question but rather a political question.

> [T]here are in effect an infinite number and variety of acts occurring in any society which may not be defined and treated as criminal. Which acts are so designated depends on the interests of the persons with sufficient political power and influence to manage to have their views prevail. Once it has been established that certain acts are to be designated as deviant, then how the laws are implemented will likewise reflect the political power of the various affected groups.[237]

Most laws derive from the activities of a relatively small minority of the population who hold positions of political and economic power.[238] As such, legislation generally promotes the interests of one group against the interest of other groups.[239] The laws that are enacted reflect the interests of those groups capable of having their views included in the official, or legal, views of society.[240] Although the groups that are most successful in having their views reflected in the laws are generally those who control both the political and the economic institutions, political success does not require both economic and political control.[241] Members of the middle class have an effect on the legislative process and often benefit from their influence on the political system—particularly on issues that threaten their economic or personal well-being. Their involvement in the political and criminal justice systems is often provoked by those things they perceive to be potential threats to their interests or benefits. The mass media plays a critical role in providing information regarding potential threats to the public.[242]

In order to understand the influence of groups such as the middle class on the legislative process, one must be familiar with the way in which legislators are selected.[243] The selection process for public officials includes their election and reelection to political office. The role of politics and the

---

236 Chambliss, 1971, 11.
237 Chambliss, 67.
238 Chambliss, 70.
239 Chambliss, 72.
240 Chambliss, 65.
241 Chambliss, 65.
242 Chambliss, 70.
243 Chambliss, 72.

politicization of crime in the United States are significant factors in the election of legislators.

Politics and Public Policy

Politics is defined in numerous ways. A simple definition is the pursuit of power by politicians, those who run for elected office and market policy proposals that resonate with enough voters to get them elected and hopefully reelected.[244]

> Politics also refers to the relations of power and influence that occur between, on the one hand, those who are professionally involved—either in the private or the public sector—in the prevention of the crimes, or in the processing of the accused and convicted and, on the other hand, those who are part of the complex representative decision-making apparatus that is called the political system in this country. This political system includes the public as electors, their representatives in the legislative bodies at all levels of government, and their elected representatives in executive positions.[245]

Politics often guides the type and substance of the policy initiatives advanced by legislators in response to the public pressure and/or personal goals of the legislators who wish to be elected or reelected. This relationship is further described by William Chambliss and Robert Seidman[246] in their description of the interaction of politics and pressure and the development of norms and sanctions. They propose that "other societal and personal forces" that influence the rule-making institutions (i.e., legislatures and legislators) include the pressure exerted by the public on legislators, as well as personal interests in their bids for reelection and to remain in positions of power. These pressures are also experienced by rule-sanctioning institutions and individuals (i.e., courts, judges, law enforcement agencies, and police rank and file) and the role-occupant (i.e., the person who is or whose behavior is targeted by the legislation, laws, and policies). The bureaucracies and their agents, therefore, have personal and organizational agendas that influence their implementation of the laws and policies.[247] These personal agendas and societal forces assist

244 Kevin Stenson. "Making Sense of Crime Control." *The Politics of Crime Control.* Ed. Kevin Stenson and David Cowell. (Newbury Park: Sage, 1991), 8.

245 Erika S. Fairchild and Vincent J. Webb. "Introduction: Crime, Justice, and Politics in the United States Today." *The Politics of Crime and Criminal Justice.* Ed. Erika S. Fairchild and Vincent J. Webb (Beverly Hills, CA: Sage, 1985), 7.

246 Chambliss and Seidman, 1971,12.

247 Chambliss and Seidman, 1971.

in explaining why public policies regarding crime are often inconsistent. When crime is politicized, the responses and initiatives that ensue are not always consistent with fact and the findings of research. Particularly during election periods, the policies are tailored to garner the support of the public. The public's response to crime, or rather their fear of crime, is culturally determined.[248]

The Politicization of Crime

Crime is a political issue. As such, politicians often exploit the public's predisposition toward crime and punishment in order to gain political office.[249] Both their actual experiences and their perceived threat of victimization inform the public's predisposition toward certain feelings about crime. The media's portrayal of the prevalence and perpetrators of crime often enhances the public's fear of victimization. Some politicians who are in need of a campaign theme choose crime, or law and order, because these are topics that engage the public's emotions and consequently have strong political value.

The politicization of crime is currently a major factor involved in the acquisition and retention of elected office. The contemporary process of the politicization of crime began with the Republican Party and Senator Barry Goldwater's 1964 presidential campaign . Although he was unsuccessful in his bid for election, Goldwater raised the issue of crime in the streets as a major political theme. When President Richard M. Nixon was elected in 1972, public opinion polls indicated for the first time in twenty years that "crime, lawlessness, looting, and rioting" were perceived by 29 percent of those asked as the "most important problems facing the nation." Fifty-two percent of those who responded identified the Vietnam War as the most important problem, and 20 percent said race relations was the most important issue.[250] The efforts of conservative politicians to politicize crime were advanced by the media's coverage of crime and law enforcement. After the early seventies, the political attention paid to crime subsided for a while. As a consequence, crime was not listed as a priority in public opinion polls again until 1980 when "drugs" became the new indicator of the respondents' concern with crime.[251]

Part of the attractiveness of crime as a political issue, and the punitive response to crime in the United States, is grounded in U.S. culture. Scheingold explains:

---

248   Scheingold, 1984.
249   Scheingold, 1984, 38; Beckett and Sasson, 2000.
250   Chambliss, 1995, 247.
251   Chambliss, 248.

What is operative is a complex and unpredictable process in which politicians seeking to obtain or retain office capitalize on public anxieties, which are only tenuously linked to the actual incidence of crime. In sum, the politics of law and order is best understood in terms of political conflict, which is shaped, to a significant degree, by the powerful symbols of American culture that determine how we understand the world around us.[252]

Scheingold provides an explanation of how crime is politicized and the role that fear of crime plays in the development of criminal justice policies. Scheingold posits that the process begins with increased crime and/or increased media attention to crime. Increased crime leads to victimization as well as increased attention by the media to crime. This increased attention from the media partly explains the sense of victimization that is experienced vicariously by some individuals. The politicization process includes politicians' response when they use the public's fear of crime to advance their campaigns by promising and/or enacting policies that will allegedly impact crime. This attention to crime by politicians also induces the media to continue or increase its focus on crime, thus causing the public to become more fearful of crime and the alleged culprits. Whether or not the responses to the fear of crime will be punitive or nonpunitive is culturally determined. The emotions and values that are incorporated into the public's thinking about crime are determinant factors.[253] Politics determine if the policy initiatives will be punitive or nonpunitive.

Law in Action: Self-Serving Agendas

Although the law represents the values and interests of powerful elements in the stratification system of complex societies, it is created specifically for and enforced by bureaucratic organizations with their own specific desires for results.[254] These organizations include legislatures, courts, and law enforcement agencies; they are part of a self-serving system designed to maintain power and privilege.[255] There is a tendency to operate in a manner that will provide the least strain and greatest reward to the organization, all with the purpose of promoting the agency's agenda. The bureaucracies tend to punish those who

---

252 Scheingold, 1984, 79.
253 Scheingold, 1984, 56.
254 Lilly, Cullen and Ball, 1995,152.
255 Chambliss and Seidman, 1971, 4.

are the least powerful because there is less strain on the bureaucracy to do so (no one can fight back) and there is less incentive not to do so.[256]

> The most salient characteristic of organizational behavior is that the ongoing policies and activities are those designed to maximize rewards and minimize strains for the organization.... This general principle is reflected in the fact that in the administration of the criminal law *those persons are arrested, tried, and sentenced who can offer the fewest rewards for nonenforcement of the laws and who can be processed without creating any undue strain* for the organizations which comprise the legal system.[257]

Bureaucracies that are comprised of elements of the criminal justice system therefore tend to treat those of lower social classes harsher than middle-class and upper-class persons for committing the same offenses because they have little to offer in return for leniency. These bureaucracies tend to ignore or deal leniently with the same offenses when committed by those higher in the stratification hierarchy.[258] Critical theorists suggest that harsh treatment is imposed on the powerless because of their inability to mount resistance. Treating the powerful in a harsh manner is avoided because of the strain their resistance would exert against the organization.[259] Policing provides an example of how law enforcement agencies operate in a class-based society. "The nature of policing in a class-based society inevitably leads to policing the poor and minorities rather than those in social classes capable of creating problems if they are heavily policed."[260] "Police departments across the nation police the urban underclass ghetto with a vigilance that would create political revolution were the same tactics and policies implemented in White [*sic*] middle-class communities."[261]

These perspectives predict that the prostitutes and not the johns will be most often arrested; children of middle-class parents who live in the suburbs will be taken home after the police or school administrators discover them committing delinquent acts while children from urban areas and of lower economic status are taken to the police station; and efforts to arrest people from affluent communities (for example, those in northern New Jersey who drove to Harlem, New York, to buy drugs) will be short-lived. Citizens

---

256 Chambliss and Seidman, 1971.
257 Chambliss 1969, 84–85.
258 Chambliss, 153.
259 Lilly, Cullen, Ball, 1995, 154–155.
260 Chambliss, 1995, 256.
261 Chambliss, 250.

who use their political power to vote, contact their elected and appointed representatives, and in other ways exert their political strength, are treated differently by law enforcement and other members of the criminal justice system than poor, disenfranchised people.

Chambliss's law, order, and power theory provides one explanation of the possible relationship between the war on drugs and the incarceration of black females. The war on drugs was presented as a way to address the drug kingpins and sellers of large amounts of crack cocaine. Instead, it has been a war against users and low-level dealers of crack cocaine.[262] Some researchers allege that politicians developed the policies that constituted the war because they wanted to be reelected to their positions of power in 1986 and 1988.[263] They targeted crack cocaine because of the media's timely focus on crack cocaine and the media's representations about the alleged dangers of crack.[264] The politicians also targeted crack because of its representations in the media and the public's belief that the users of crack cocaine were primarily black people who lived in urban areas and who threatened the safety of white people who lived in suburban areas.[265]

The media paid special attention to black females who used crack.[266] These women were often portrayed as promiscuous—exhibiting behavior that contradicted the norms of white mainstream society. They were also depicted as giving indiscriminate birth to "crack babies" who were fated to suffer from neurological and behavioral problems all of their lives. This depiction of black females who used crack made them appear to be people who promoted lifestyles that were threats to both societal norms and the economic well-being of taxpayers who would then be required to pay for the care and treatment of these children.[267] Black females were easy targets of these drug policies because of their marginalized and relatively powerless position in society.[268] They did not have economic or political power. Politicians were not concerned that the people who were targeted would have the ability to challenge the drug

---

262 United States Sentencing Commission. *Special Report to the Congress: Cocaine and Federal Sentencing Policy.* (Washington, DC: US Government Printing Office, 2007 and 1995).

263 Katherine Beckett and Theodore Sasson. *The Politics of Injustice.* (California: Pine Forge Press, 2000).

264 Beckett and Sasson, 2000; Craig Reinarman and Henry Levine. "The Crack Attack: Politics and the Media in the Crack Scare." *Crack in America.* (Berkeley: University Press, 1997).

265 Drew Humphries. *Crack Mothers.* (Ohio: Ohio State University Press, 1999).; Reinarman and Levine, 1997.

266 Humphries, 1999.

267 Humphries, 1999.

268 Bell Hooks. Ain't I A Woman. (Boston, MA: South End Press, 1981).; Vilma Ortiz. "Women of Color: A Demographic Overview." *Women of Color in U.S. Society.* (Philadelphia, PA: Temple University Press, 1994).

policies. The targets of the legislation, in this instance black females, were viewed as "others" against whom the voting public would rally. The harsh sanctions instituted for low level-offenses involving crack cocaine would not create strain on the legislative body or legislators because those who were targeted would not have the political or economic resources to respond to the political pressures and cause problems.[269] Legislators would be rewarded for appearing to have dealt with the crime problem in an effective manner that protected the resources of the groups who voted for them and financed their political campaigns.

Summary of the Conflict Perspectives

In summary, the conflict theories focus upon the struggle for resources that exists because of the stratification of society. These resources include interests, such as status, power, and material well-being, and values, which include norms and moral differences within society.[270] The conflict theories of law, order, and power,[271] and the cultural interpretation of the politics of crime[272] theorize that:

1. Laws incorporate the norms and values of groups that are able to influence the legislative process;[273]

2. The groups that have influence over the political system have economic and/or political power;[274]

3. Because of the politicization of crime, some groups have political power without economic power;[275]

4. When able, groups exercise their political influence in order to protect their interests, including their material and physical well-being. They do this by exerting pressure on elected officials to initiate policies that they believe will protect their interests;[276]

5. Crime has been politicized because of the fear of crime experienced by the public. (The impetus of such fear is the result of actual and/or vicarious victimization.);[277]

---

269   Chambliss, 1971.
270   Scheingold, 1984, 224.
271   Chambliss and Seidman, 1971.
272   Scheingold, 1984.
273   Chambliss and Seidman, 1984.
274   Chambliss and Seidman, 1984.
275   Chambliss and Seidman, 1984.
276   Scheingold, 1984.
277   Scheingold, 1984.

6. The representation of crime and criminals by the media is both the cause and result of the public's fear of crime and the politiciation of crime;[278] and

7. The policies that are enacted by legislators, sanctioned by judges and prosecutors, and enforced by law enforcement agencies, result from societal and personal pressures exerted on each agency/agent and are political and self-serving in nature.[279]

How do these perspectives inform our investigation into the relationship between the war on drugs and black women? To determine how they may do so, we must first have an understanding of the status of black women in the United States.

Anti-Essentialism: The Inextricable State of Being a Black Female

The concept of essentialism originated in the early 1900s as an educational theory. It stated that ideas and skills that are basic to a culture should be taught to all persons, using accepted, proven methods of instruction.[280] Since, then the term *essentialism* has evolved to mean many things. In a postmodernist approach to the study of criminology, particularly in feminist criminology, essentialism is the concept that *one* "authentic female or minority 'voice' exists"[281] for all issues. Essentialism assumes that all women, regardless of their race or ethnicity, experience the same social realities, disregarding the effect of socialization and the societal expectations that are placed upon people because of their various races and ethnicities. Adherence to monolithic essentialism based upon race or gender subordinates the experiences of black females to those of their male counterparts and female counterparts of other races. Furthermore, it contradicts historical and contemporary reality. Marcia Rice underscores the complexity of the experience of black women in her argument against essentialism in criminal justice research:[282]

> The experiences of Black women as chattels under slavery and colonialism has meant that social relations were often mediated

---

278 Scheingold, 1984.

279 Chambliss and Seidman, 1984.

280 Webster. *Merriam-Webster's Collegiate Dictionary 10th Ed.* Springfield, MA: Merriam-Webster Inc., 1993.

281 Adrien K. Wing. "Essentialism and Anti-Essentialism: Ain't I a Woman?" *Critical Race Feminism*. Ed. Adrien K. Wing. (New York, NY: New York University, 1997), 7.

282 Marcia Rice. "Challenging orthodoxies in feminist theory: a black feminist critique." *Feminist Perspectives in Criminology*. Ed. Loraine Gelsthorpe and Allison Morris. (Bristol, PA: Open University Press, 1992).

and bound up with economic as much as sexual reproduction. Thus, to understand the unique oppression of Black women, we need to consider their experiences as Black people.… Black women experience sexual and patriarchal oppression by Black men, but at the same time, struggle alongside them against racial oppression.[283]

Tonry appropriately acknowledged that the experiences of black males as they relate to the war on drug initiatives are different from those of black females, and he conducted the study in a somewhat nonessentialist manner.[284] In doing so, he restricted his research solely to evaluating the impact of the 1987–1988 drug law initiatives of the federal government on the incarceration of black males. He explained his rationale for doing so thusly:

> Racial disproportions are about as bad in women's prisons as in men's. Like men, about half of female prisoners are Black. However, women make up only 6 to 7 percent of the total number of prisoners. Because one of my central arguments is that by removing so many young Black men from their families and communities, crime control policies are undermining efforts to ameliorate the conditions of life of the Black urban underclass, the focus on Black men is necessary. *The story of Black women as offenders and as prisoners is important, but it is a different story.*[285] (Italics added.)

The story of many black female offenders and prisoners is important *and* is different from that of black males and white females. As is the case with black males, the imprisonment of women also has a profound effect on the family and the community. However, even this impact is different because, unlike their male counterparts, most female inmates were responsible for the care of a child or children at the time of their arrest or imprisonment.[286]

In criminology, most research that focuses on race focuses on black males. Until recently, the standard used in the study of gender and criminal justice has concentrated on white females. These approaches to the treatment of race and gender adhere to the essentialist view that there is a racially monolithic experience, that is, the experience of black males, as well as a sexually monolithic experience as lived by white females. Adhering to a racially monolithic version of reality implies that the social constructs of gender are unimportant factors

---

283 Rice, 63–64.
284 Tonry, 1995.
285 Tonry, 1995, ix.
286 American Correctional Association. *The Female Offender: What Does the Future Hold?* (Washington, DC: St. Mary's Press, 1990).

that do not influence persons within the same racial groups differently. This would mean that the experiences of a black female are not different from those of a black male and that their gender differences are inconsequential or are substantively insignificant. Understandably, the experience of black males in the criminal justice system is the subject of many criminologists' research; the disproportionate number of black males who are arrested and incarcerated requires explanation. However, when it is assumed that the experiences of black males can be extrapolated to that of black females, the leap is made without justification. At times, black females have been overrepresented among women in the criminal justice system to a greater extent than black males among incarcerated men.[287] Racial essentialism cannot be substantiated by the facts. Although the experiences of black women and men have been similar due to the commonality of their race, their gender differences are also major forces in their life experiences. American society is based not only on the tenets of white supremacy, but just as importantly, on patriarchy.[288]

Gender essentialism proposes that all women have the same attributes and capabilities. It assumes that "a unitary, 'essential' women's experience can be isolated and described independently of race, class, sexual orientation, and other realties of experience."[289]

One common critique of feminist theorists is that they assumed previously that the experiences of middle-class white women were the norm for all women, including women of color. Some feminist criminologists have acknowledged that one cannot include the experiences of black women into feminist theories (or any theories) by simply adding "color and stir[ring]."[290] In the 1990s, feminist post-modernists or post-structuralists began to focus more attention on the differences among women and among races. Most contemporary feminists acknowledge the inaccuracy of essentialism and attempts to incorporate anti-essentialist methods of research and analyses.[291]

Critical race feminism rejects essentialism and emphasizes theoretical and practical considerations of race, gender, and class in the study of the lives of women of color.[292] The premise of this perspective is that there is no monolithic "women's experience" that can be understood without regard

---

287 BJS, 1999.
288 Hooks, 1981.
289 A.P. Harris. "Race and Essentialism in Feminist Legal Theory." *Stanford Legal Review* 42 (1990): 585.
290 Sally Simpson. "Feminist Theory, Crime, and Justice." *Criminology* 27.4 (1989): 605–631.
291 Kathleen Daly and Lisa Maher. "Crossroads and Intersections: Building from Feminist Critique." *Criminology at the Crossroads.* Ed. Kathleen Daly and Lisa Maher. (New York, NY: Oxford University Press, 1998) 1.
292 Wing, 1997, 7.

to other factors such as race, class, and sexual orientation. The assumption that there is but one black, Hispanic, or white experience is rejected.[293] The consequence of assuming an anti-essentialist position is that black women are no longer seen simply as intersections of their race and gender. Instead of fragmenting and dissecting the black woman from her racial or sexual identity, critical race feminism acknowledges and understands that she is one entity and neither her race nor her gender can be subtracted, divided, or extracted from her being. She is inextricably a black female.

The Marginalized Status of Black Females in the United States

The characteristics of being both black and female position black women into two groups that have had immense growth in their contact with the criminal justice system.[294] It has been postulated that the treatment of black women by the criminal justice system actually mirrors the social and historical experiences of black women in the United States. Vernetta Young articulates the characterizations used to describe black American women:[295]

> As an Amazon ... she is domineering, assertive and masculine.... *In the case of the Black female offender, there is no need for the criminal justice system to protect her by keeping her out of jail or prison or by giving her shorter sentences, because she can take care of herself. She will not be harmed by these harsh dispositions.* On the other hand, if she is a Black female victim of wife-battering, there is no need to intervene, because she is inherently violent, and again capable of protecting herself. As a "sinister sapphire," ... she is treacherous toward and contemptuous of Black men, dangerous and castrating. *As a Black female offender, she is deserving of harsher dispositions.* On the other hand, if she is a Black female rape victim, she is ... vindictive and is not a believable complainant. A Black female battering victim ... deserves the violence perpetrated upon her because she precipitated it.... The Black mammy ... is a long-suffering paragon of patience. *[As a] ... Black female offender, this suggests that she can endure incarceration, so there is no need to focus on alternatives.* As a seductress, then, she is loose, immoral, and sexually depraved. As a Black female rape victim, she cannot be a legitimate victim. She precipitated her

---

293   Angela Harris. "Race and Essentialism in Feminist Legal Theory." *Critical Race Feminism.* Ed. Adrien Katherine Wing. (New York: New York University Press, 1997) 11.

294   Mauer and Huling, 1995.

295   Vernetta Young. "Gender Expectations and Their Impact on Black Female Offenders and Their Victims." *Justice Quarterly* 3.2: 305–327.

victimization and deserves the violence perpetrated against her.[296] (Italics added.)

The United States was developed and, some argue, continues to operate as a white supremacist patriarchal capitalist society.[297] White males are central to the power structure in the United States. The more unlike white males a person is, the further he or she is from the center of power. Although black males share a common sex with white men, and white females share a racial identity with white men, by virtue of their element of difference, they too are often precluded from occupying positions of power. (It is important to note that in 2008 the United States elected its first African American president, Barack Obama. Time will tell if this marks the beginning of a postracial society and how that will impact the status of black women.) Farthest from the center and situated in the farthest margins of the power structure are black women. Their experiences in the United States, both historically and contemporaneously, reflect their status as neither white nor male, and they are therefore relegated to the margins of power.[298]

Historically, black women were brought to the United States for the sole purpose of providing labor for white males and their families. As slaves, black females were devalued as human beings, women, and mothers.[299] Although both black women and black men suffered harsh experiences as slaves, their experiences were different. Female slaves suffered death and beatings along with their men, while their slave owners also subjected them to rape for both sexual pleasure and to impregnate them for the economic benefit of the white slave owners. Enslaved black people also accepted the patriarchal definitions of their gender roles.[300] Black females were required to complete their labor in the fields as well as to fulfill their "feminine duties" of providing homes within their slave quarters. Black women were required to give birth to children irrespective of how they had been fathered. Their motherhood was devalued as their babies were often taken and sold for the benefit of the slave owner.[301]

Black females and white females have never had equal social status.[302] During slavery, black slaves viewed white females as being placed on pedestals by their husbands, families, and slave owners. Conversely, white women were

296 Young, 323.
297 Hooks, 1995.
298 Hooks, 1995.
299 Bell Hooks. *Ain't I A Woman*. (Boston, MA: South End Press, 1981).
300 Hooks, 47; Herbert G. Gutman. *The Black Family in Slavery and Freedom, 1750–1925*. (New York, NY: Vintage Books, 1976) 350.
301 Harriet A. Jacobs. *Incidents in the Life of a Slave Girl Written by Herself*. (Cambridge, MA: Harvard University Press, 1987); Gutman, 1976.
302 Freda Adler. *Sisters in Crime*. (New York, NY: McGraw Hill, 1975) 133–154.

considered the property of their husbands and were often subjected to marital rape, forced to bear children, and made to accept the fact that their husbands fathered children with women and girls who were slaves.[303] Throughout these demeaning and humiliating experiences, white females continued to assume a position of power far above that of the powerless black female. White females enjoyed the privileges of their whiteness, and although not male, during slavery they assumed a position of power and freedom in the social hierarchy above that of black females and black males.

During the women's movements, white females used their race as a point from which to argue for their equality with their male counterparts. During the fight for suffrage, some white males supported the idea that black males should be given the right to vote to the exclusion of all women. Some white females exploited their racial status and argued that they, and not black males, should be afforded the right to vote.[304]

Black females have always been marginalized in American society by virtue of their race and sex. Even today, with all of the advancements that women and minorities have made, black women still occupy the lower rungs of the socioeconomic ladder. For example, in the 1980s, during the time that the Anti-Drug Abuse Acts were enacted, only 51.5 percent of black females in the United States had graduated from high school, while during the same period, 68.1 percent of white females had graduated. In 1980, 13.3 percent of white females were college graduates as compared to 8.3 percent of black females.[305] In 1988, black women led 42.3 percent of the female-headed families in the United States. White females were the heads of 12.9 percent of the female-headed households. Generally, families headed by women have lower income levels and tend to be poorer than households with two parents. However, in 1987, 51.8 percent of the families headed by black women were considered to be living in poverty compared to 26.7 percent of similarly situated white females.[306]

By the dawn of the twenty-first century, black women still remained marginalized, and in 2005, African American women continued to experience the highest poverty rate in the United States. Twenty-five percent of African American women were living in poverty as compared to 10 percent of white women, 23 percent of Hispanic women, 10 percent of white males, 17 percent of black males, and 16 percent of Hispanic males.[307] Black women

---

303 Jacobs, 1987.

304 Hooks, 1981, 3.

305 Vilma Ortiz. "Women of Color: A Demographic Overview" *Women of Color in U.S. Society.* Ed. Maxine Baca Zinn and Bonnie Thornton Dill. (Philadelphia, PA: Temple University Press,1994), 26.

306 Ortiz, 1994.

307 U.S. Department of Commerce, Bureau of the Census, 2005 American Community Survey, calculated by the Institute for Women's Policy Research.

(29.1 percent) made up the greatest percentage of women who were heads of households in 2004, followed by Hispanic women (16.4 percent) and white women (9.0 percent). Female-headed households continued to represent the largest percentage of adults in families living in poverty.[308] The marginalized status of African American females was explained by Amy Caiazza, April Shaw, and Misha Werschkul, as being rooted in "persistent discrimination in hiring and promotion, occupational segregation by race and gender, and differences in access to higher education."[309]

Prior Research on the Sentencing of Black Females

Unfortunately, relatively few criminologists have studied the criminality of black females and the treatment of black females within the criminal justice system. Consequently, there is little understanding of the combined effects of race and gender on the treatment of black women within the criminal justice system. As noted by Mauer and Huling in their attempt to explain why black females experienced the greatest increase in criminal justice control of all demographic groups studied, "Although research on women of color in the criminal justice system is limited, existing data and research suggest it is the combination of race and sex effects that is at the root of the trends which appear in our data."[310] Existing studies support Mauer and Huling's position and have found that black and white females are treated differently at every stage of the criminal justice system.[311, 312]

For decades, researchers consistently concluded that the black female has experienced harsher treatment than white females in the criminal justice

---

308   U.S. Department of Health and Human Services, Health resources and Services Administration. *Women's Health USA 2006*. Rockville, Maryland: U.S. Department of Health and Human Services, 2006. pp 14–15.

309   Amy Caiazza, April Shaw, and Misha Werschkul. "Women's Economic Status in the States: Wide Disparities by Race, Ethnicity, and Region." (Washington, DC Institute for Women's Policy Research) 20.

310   Mauer and Huling, 1995, 18.

311   Kathleen Daly. "Structure and Practice of Familial-based Justice in the Criminal Court." *Law and Society Review*, 21.2 (1987): 267–290.

-------"Neither Conflict nor Labeling nor Paternalism will Suffice: Intersections of Race, Ethnicity, Gender and Family in Criminal Court Decisions." *Crime and Delinquency* 35.1(1989): 136–168.

-------. Gender, Crime and Punishment. (New Haven, CT: Yale University Press, 1994).

Cora Mae Richey Mann. "Minority and Female: A Criminal Justice Double Bind," *Social Justice* 16.4 (1989): 95; Mann 1995.

312   Adler (1975) found in her study conducted in the early 1970s in Philadelphia, that there were no significant differences between the races in bail decisions and case dispositions. It should be noted that this research preceded the war on drugs.

system, from the decision to arrest through sentencing. Visher concluded from her observational study of arrests by police in various cities that chivalrous treatment tends not to be displayed toward the black female.[313] Instead, white female suspects who are older and submissive receive the preferential treatment afforded by chivalry. Simpson confirmed these findings in her review of the literature from 1984 through 1989.[314] Police were found to extend preferential treatment to white women as opposed to black women, married women received more lenient sentences than did single women, and women with families were treated with more leniency than women who had no families. Part of the explanation for the disparity in treatment may be explained by the fact that more black females tend to be single. Omolola Omole also found that gender statuses impacted the pretrial release dispositions of federal defendants, particularly for the black females in her sample.[315]

In a study of the populations of jailed females in Florida, New York, and California, Cora Mae Richey Mann confirmed that one-third of these prisoners were being detained for drug offenses.[316] When differentiated by race, 32.2 percent of the white females and 33.8 percent of the black females were being held for drug offenses. Mann reported that the white female drug offenders tended to be jailed for drug trafficking; however, the black female drug offenders were most often detained for the lower-level offense of drug possession.

Mann noted the virtually unlimited discretion exercised by prosecutors in their determination of who would be charged or not charged at the very beginning of the processing of a criminal case.[317] This unbridled discretion increases the likelihood that minorities will be "charged, overcharged, and indicted." Cassia Spohn, John Gruhl, and Susan Welch studied the prosecutors' rejection or dismissal of charges in felony cases in Los Angeles.[318] Controlling for the defendants' ages, prior criminal records, seriousness of the charges, and use of weapons, these researchers found that both white females and white males had higher rates of rejection of their charges at the initial stages, whereas, the racial and ethnic minority suspects and defendants did

---

313 Christy Visher. "Gender, Police Arrest Decisions, and Notions of Chivalry." *Criminology* 21.1 (1983): 5–28.

314 Simpson, 1989.

315 Omolola Esther Omole. *Clarifying the Role of Gender in the Court Dispositions: A LISREL Model of Pretrial Release.* (Michigan: UMI Press, 1991).

316 Mann, 1995.

317 Mann, 1993.

318 Cassi Spohn, John Gruhl, and Susan Welch. "The Impact of the Ethnicity and Gender of Defendants on the Decision to Reject or Dismiss Felony Charges." *Criminology* 25.1(1987): 175–191.

not. They also noted that white females had a notably lower rate of prosecution (19 percent) than black females (30 percent).

Linda Foley and Christine Rasche analyzed data covering a sixteen-year period in Missouri in order to investigate the effects of race on the sentencing of defendants.[319] They concluded that, in general, the black women in their study received longer (55.1 months) sentences than the white women (52.5 months) for the same crimes. They also discovered that although white women received longer sentences (182.3 months) for personal crimes than their black counterparts (98.5 months), the latter group actually served more time for these offenses (black women: 26.7 months; white women: 23 months). These two groups showed no significant difference in mean sentences for drug offenses; however, once again, the black women served more time (20.4 months against 13.2 months for white women).

Candace Kruttschnitt reviewed outcomes of sentencing for 1,034 female defendants in a northern California county from 1972 to 1976.[320] She concluded that black females who were convicted of drug offenses or disturbing the peace received harsher sentences than their white counterparts. Approximately eighteen years later in 1990, Mann compared the arrest rates to the imprisonment data for women in California, New York, and Florida, who were charged with major felonies (drug violations, theft, burglary, and robbery).[321] Mann found that women of color who were arrested for these crimes were sentenced to prison more often than white women with similar arrests. Furthermore, she determined that California, the state that incarcerates more women than any other state in the nation and that also has a larger population of incarcerated females than any other government in the world, appears to differentiate among these women based upon race. Mann pointed out that most of the women who are arrested for violations of drug laws are white (48.3 percent) as compared to black (30.5 percent) or Hispanic women (18.7 percent). However, disparity exists in the percentages of those who are sentenced to prison. White female drug offenders constitute only 38.3 percent of those who were sentenced to prison, as compared to 34.1 percent for black and 26.1 percent for Hispanic American female drug law violators.[322] Unfortunately, Mann was unable to control for the prior records of the female felons in this study. She did state, however, that with such controls she would still expect to find evidence of disparate treatment. Mann

319 Linda A. Foley and Christine E. Rasche. "The Effect of Race on Sentence, Actual Time Served and Final Disposition of Female Offenders." *Theory and Research in Criminal Justice*. Ed. John A. Conley. (Cincinnati, OH: Anderson Press, 1979).

320 Candace Kruttschnitt. 1980–1981. "Social Status and Sentences of Female Offenders." *Law and Society* 15.2 (1980–1981):247–265.

321 Mann, 1995.

322 Mann, 1995, 128.

posited that it would be implausible that prior arrests could impact the three racial/ethnic groups in the three separate states in such a way as to explain away the disparity in sentencing.[323]

The statistics presented indicate that the presence of black women prisoners accounted for the largest increase in the growth of the prison population that occurred during the 1980s and 1990s. Both their race and their gender appear to have exacerbated their situation. As discussed earlier in this chapter, black women shared the media spotlight with black men in the 1980s as they were both held out to be the culprits of the so-called crack epidemic. They were portrayed as "others": inner-city dwellers, addicted to crack, sexually promiscuous, and giving birth to crack babies.[324] Consequently, black women were easy targets for the politically derived drug policies contained within the Anti-Drug Abuse Acts of 1986 and 1988.[325] Based upon the prior research and data, one should not be surprised by the findings in the present study that indicate how the drug war has impacted black women and has been allowed to do so for so long.

Unfortunately, based upon their marginalized status in the United States, lack of political power, socioeconomic status, and racial and gender juxtaposition, black women have been allowed to be targeted by the Anti-Drug Abuse Acts of 1986 and 1988 with decades of unjust punishment and with little or no attention paid to their plight. As with all actions, there are consequences. The consequences of incarcerating black women with draconian sentences have had direct and collateral consequences on the women, their families, children, communities, and society. If they began as unintended victims, I submit that at some point, with the clear evidence of how they were being snared in the system for low-level drug offenses involving crack, the unintentional became intentional.

So, what does it matter anyway? What were the consequences of incarcerating so many black women for so long and for so little reason? In the next chapter, some of the direct and collateral consequences will be discussed.

---

323 Mann, 1995, 129.

324 Steven R. Belenko. *Crack and the Evolution of Anti-Drug Policy.* (Westport, CT: Greenwood Press, 1993); USSC, 1995, 1997; Inciardi, Lockwood, Pottieger, 1993; Humphries, 1999.

325 Humphries, 1999; Beckett and Sasson, 2000.

CHAPTER NINE

What Does It Matter Anyway?: Impacts on the Women, Their Families, and Their Communities

My purpose for writing this book was to analyze the impact of the war on drugs, which I defined as the Anti-Drug Abuse Acts of 1986 and 1988 (ADAAs), on the incarceration of black women convicted of drug offenses involving crack cocaine. I also wanted to determine if and how the impact has changed in the more than twenty years since the enactment of this federal legislation. This research was prompted first by the disproportionate representation of black females among the population of incarcerated females in general, and among women incarcerated for drug offenses specifically, and second, by the tremendous growth in the percentage of black females who were incarcerated for drug offenses between 1986 and 1991. Although some criminologists have proposed that the war on drugs has caused the increased incarceration of women in general,[326] only a few have suggested that black females are particularly impacted by the drug law initiatives.[327] This increase in the imprisonment of black women does not tend to attract the attention of criminologists, policy-makers, and the public, as has the incarceration of black men, and women in general, although both the impact and consequences are of equal importance.

Most of the research to date has been descriptive in nature and therefore provided important information about the black women who are incarcerated for drug offenses, but this research did not test the significance of various factors that may explain black women's disproportionate representation within the population of female drug offenders. The goal of this research was to get a

---

326 Chesney-Lind, 1995; Feinman, 1994.
327 For example: Mauer and Huling, 1995.

better idea of how the mandatory minimum sentencing and the low threshold amounts of crack cocaine that trigger the mandatory minimums have been affecting the likelihood and length of prison sentences given to women, particularly black women, convicted of crack cocaine offenses in the federal system. Now that more than twenty years have passed since the enactment of the Anti-Drug Abuse Acts of 1986 and 1988, an additional goal was to determine what, if anything, has changed about how black women convicted of crack cocaine offenses are affected by these elements of the federal drug policies.

Although it was not anticipated at the outset of this study that the war on drugs would provide a complete explanation for the overrepresentation of black women in the general population of incarcerated females, it was predicted that focusing on the subpopulation of women who are incarcerated for drug offenses would provide important information about the disproportionate commitment of black women in the federal prison system. This stance is based on the fact that drug offenses constitute the single largest homogeneous group of offenses for which women are imprisoned in the federal system. Therefore, information that can be gleaned about the factors that influence the overrepresentation of black females within this key category should lead to an understanding about the disproportionate representation of black women within the general population of incarcerated women as a whole and the impact of the drug policies on the incarceration of black women. Furthermore, understanding the relationship between crack cocaine and the incarceration of black females is important in and of itself, and the policy implications beg to be addressed.

Summary of Findings

The federal system was the jurisdiction selected for this policy impact analysis because few states enacted drug policies that were as ominous as those of the federal government, although some did incorporate elements such as differential treatment of offenses involving the different forms of cocaine, crack and powdered. The 100:1 ratio for powdered cocaine as compared to crack cocaine, as established by the federal laws, was also a reason for focusing on the federal level. Previous research has concentrated on the impact of this disparity on the punishment of black males, but the impact on black females has not been addressed.

The war on drugs was defined as the application of mandatory minimum sentencing to drug offenses involving crack cocaine. The war on drugs was conceptualized in this manner because of the history of the federal drug initiatives, their focus on crack cocaine, the media representation of crack cocaine abusers, and the policing techniques used for the enforcement of these drug initiatives.

The Impact of the War on Drugs Then and Now

The primary questions for this policy analysis are stated below.

Primary Question One

What influence did crack cocaine and downward departures have on the sentencing of black females who were convicted of drug offenses that required a mandatory minimum sentence?

Primary Question Two

Did the influences of crack cocaine and downward departures on the sentencing of black females for drug offenses involving crack cocaine change between 1996 and 2006?

Several descriptive and multivariate analyses were performed on the data. The findings indicate that the legislative initiatives contained in the Anti-Drug Abuse Acts of 1986 and 1988 had and continue to have a significant impact on black women's imprisonment for drug offenses in the federal criminal justice system.

In the federal system, black women are convicted of and sentenced for drug offenses that involve crack cocaine more often than any other drug. Black females are also convicted for crack cocaine offenses more often than are other women. In these samples, 50.8 percent and 42.5 percent of black women who were convicted of drug offenses in 1996 and 2006, respectively, were convicted of offenses that involved crack cocaine. Furthermore, 75.8 percent and 57.6 percent of all women who were convicted of crack offenses in 1996 and 2006, respectively, were black females. This is consistent with other studies that have found that although most users of crack cocaine are white, the policing techniques used to implement the policies related to crack cocaine focus on open markets in urban areas and consequently lead to the arrest of the inhabitants of urban areas, specifically, black females and black males.

Among all women convicted of a drug offense, convictions for crack cocaine offenses, as compared to other types of drugs, did not increase the likelihood of women in general receiving prison sentences in 1996, but did in 2006. Women who were convicted of drug offenses that involved crack cocaine in 1996 were almost half as likely (.54:1) to receive a prison sentence than if other types of drugs were involved, but by 2006 they were 1.5 times as likely (1.5:1) to receive prison sentences. Considering that black women continued to be the largest single group of women convicted of drug offenses involving crack cocaine in 2006, they were disproportionately impacted by this trend toward an increased likelihood of receiving prison sentences.

Convictions for drug offenses that involve crack cocaine did have a significant impact on the amount of prison time received by women in general. Females who were convicted of drug offenses involving crack cocaine were likely to receive prison sentences that were 29 percent longer in 1996 and 37 percent longer in 2006 than for other drugs. Black women were impacted more than the sample of all women, as black women received prison sentences that were 49 percent longer in 1996 and 99.8 percent longer in 2006, if the drug involved in their cases was crack cocaine rather than some other drug. Thus, black women who were convicted of crack cocaine offenses received much longer periods of incarceration than did white and Hispanic women who were convicted of offenses involving crack cocaine.

In 1996 the mandatory minimum sentencing schemes applied to convictions that involved crack cocaine were significant in their impact on the odds that black females would *receive prison sentences*. These black women were five times more likely to go to prison than if the drug involved was another type of drug. By 2006 a change had occurred: mandatory minimum sentencing *no longer significantly affected* the odds that black women convicted of crack cocaine offenses as opposed to other drugs would receive a prison sentence.

Conversely, mandatory minimum sentences applied to drug offenses that involved crack cocaine did have a major impact on the *length of sentences* received by black females. In this sample, black females convicted of crack cocaine offenses received prison sentences that were 84 percent longer in 1996 and 98 percent longer in 2006 than prison sentences for black females who were convicted of crack offenses but who were not sentenced using mandatory minimum sentences.

So, by 2006, although mandatory minimum sentencing no longer affected the likelihood that black women convicted of crack cocaine offenses would receive prison sentences, it did have a major impact on the length of prison sentences they received.

In summary, there were changes between 1996 and 2006 in the impact of the major components underlying the war on drugs—that is, mandatory minimum sentencing for crack offenses—on the incarceration of black women:

1. Although mandatory minimum sentencing increased the *likelihood* of incarceration among women convicted of crack cocaine offenses in 1996, it no longer did so in 2006.

2. Mandatory minimum sentencing greatly increased the *length* of prison sentences received by women convicted of crack offenses, and the effect was greater in 2006 than in 1996.

3. Being convicted of crack cocaine offenses as compared to other drug offenses increased black women's likelihood of incarceration in 2006 (which was not the case in 1996).

4. Although being convicted of crack offenses increased the length of prison terms in 1996, even longer sentences were handed down in 2006.

5. Black women convicted of crack offenses received longer sentences in both years than did white or Hispanic women who were also convicted of crack offenses.

6. Women convicted of crack offenses were more likely to receive five-year mandatory minimum sentences in 1996; that changed by 2006 when they were more likely to receive ten-year mandatory sentences.

7. Downward departures and other adjustments lessened the length of incarceration, but most black women convicted of crack cocaine offenses still received lengthy prison sentences.

The 100:1 ratio for powdered cocaine as compared to crack cocaine makes it more likely that women who are convicted of drug offenses involving crack are sentenced to prison more often and for longer periods of time than women who are convicted of drug offenses that involve powdered cocaine. Among women who are convicted of drug offenses in the federal system, it is black women who are most likely to be convicted of drug offenses involving crack, and black women are more likely to be imprisoned and sentenced for longer prison terms. Their presence in prison, as compared to their presence in the uninstitutionalized population is, and for the foreseeable future, will continue to be, disproportionate as long as the low threshold amounts of crack cocaine, as compared to powdered cocaine and other drugs, trigger statutory mandatory minimum sentences of imprisonment.

Who Are These Black Women?

To better understand the impact of the drug initiatives on black women, their families, and communities, a subsample of the black women who were convicted of drug offenses that involved crack cocaine was collected from the population used in the analyses. The constraints used were that they had little or no criminal record, had been sentenced to prison under mandatory minimum sentencing statutes, and—very important—the offenses involved less than five hundred grams of crack cocaine. This amount was chosen because it represents the threshold amount that would have been used to trigger the mandatory minimum sentence of five years if the form of cocaine was powdered cocaine instead of crack. In comparison, five-year prison sentences are triggered by five grams of crack cocaine or five hundred grams of powdered cocaine, and ten-year prison sentences are triggered by fifty grams of crack cocaine or five thousand grams of powdered cocaine.

This sample totaled 155 women. The ages of the women ranged from nineteen to fifty-eight years, with an average age of thirty-two. Most of these black women had completed the eleventh grade or all of high school. Seventy-two percent of the women had more than one dependent, and 68.8 percent had between one and three children for whom they were responsible. In fact, collectively, these women had at least 241 children for whom they were responsible prior to incarceration and who were remanded to the care of someone else, including grandparents, single parents, or the foster care system. These mothers, who had minimal or no criminal records, were convicted for an average amount of 136.18 grams and 85 grams of crack cocaine in 1996 and 2006, respectively. These amounts were far less than the 500 grams established for triggering sentences of five years for drug violations that involve *powdered* cocaine. However, these women were convicted of offenses that involved a derivative of powdered cocaine—a *less potent* form of the drug—and received average prison sentences of 70.13 months (7.8 years) in 1996 and 47 months (3 years, 11 months) in 2006.[328] In all likelihood, based upon their minimal or nonexistent criminal records and the small amounts of drugs involved, if the form of cocaine had been powdered instead of crack, these women would not have been imprisoned at all.

At the beginning of each chapter in this book, I have included a short vignette about an actual black woman who has been incarcerated in the federal prison for drug offenses involving crack cocaine. These women's stories vary in many instances; a common element is that they were all low-level actors or non-participants in the drug market, and in most instances their relationships with men who were involved in drugs is what drew them into the criminal justice system. Most reported that they were convicted of conspiracy and were used as pawns by men who were much more involved in the drug deals; as a result, the latter could receive lesser sentences for substantial assistance. Because of the males' higher-level involvement in the drug trade, as compared to the women's minimal involvement, the men were able to "roll over" on the women or provide information to the feds, true or not. In some instances, this meant the men received extremely lenient sentences while the women were sentenced to serve decades of their lives in prison. Although many of these women might not have been completely innocent of wrongdoing, when

328 See Appendix B.

I read their stories I must question how their punishment is substantiated by their involvement in the crimes for which they were convicted. Some of these women received life or several life sentences for nonviolent offenses and with no prior criminal records, while other people convicted of homicides were sentenced to serve much less time.

Among the eight women presented in this book when convicted, seven were in their twenties and one was in her early forties. Seven of the women were convicted of conspiracy and one with possession and intent to distribute crack cocaine. Each woman was involved in some way with a male (eight with husbands or boyfriends and one with her son) who was involved in the drug trade. At least half indicate they had committed no overt acts, while others said they picked up money. In many of the cases, the women reported that they did not have the information the federal agents wanted them to provide against their husbands, significant others, or family members and therefore could not offer anything, without committing perjury, in exchange for substantial assistance and a lesser sentence or none at all. At least one woman indicated she felt her life would be in danger if she provided information against the man from whom she had tried to get away. In total, among these eight women alone, there were sixteen minor children who were affected by their imprisonment. Their prison sentences ranged from ten years to three life sentences. In no case was anyone convicted of homicide or a violent offense. Many of these women are still imprisoned.

The Social Costs of Drug Policies on Black Females

The consequences of imprisoning the thousands of black women who have been incarcerated for drug offenses over the last two decades plus have been dire for the women, their families, and their communities. As black women, even without felony records or years of being locked up, they began life from a marginalized status in the United States using just about any indicator. Because of their incarcerations, the women become even more disenfranchised than they had been prior to their convictions. Based upon current laws, a felony conviction for a drug offense may present additional obstacles for a person who was formerly incarcerated that prevent or restrict them in a number of areas.

- Living in public housing: Because of black women's economic status upon returning to their communities, and their often weakened family ties, public housing may be the only affordable option these women have for decent housing. Many states have passed laws that forbid anyone with a drug felony from living in public housing or visiting for an extended period. This prevents some of the women from being able to regain custody of their children or be safe and hold down jobs.

- Attending certain colleges: Some states have passed legislation that prevents ex-offenders from attending their state colleges and universities. Education is necessary to enable a person to gain the skills needed for today's jobs and to be able to attain and maintain meaningful, legal employment.

- Certain types of employment: Being an ex-offender can prevent a person from obtaining certification or working in various occupations. Some of these areas of employment have been traditionally occupied by women and include, but are not limited to, caring for children, caring for the elderly, and cosmetology.

- Attaining certain licenses: In some states ex-offenders may find it difficult to renew their driver's licenses thus making it difficult to get to work or school and to fulfill other obligations.

- Receiving Medicaid and healthcare: This provides another barrier to some ex-offenders to becoming or staying healthy. This can impact the individuals, their families, and their communities.

- Receiving food stamps or general assistance: When such assistance is not provided to people with drug felonies, it makes it almost impossible for them to bridge the financial gap during the time they are seeking employment.

- Voting: In many states, ex-offenders are either not allowed to vote or have to go through an application process to reinstate their voting rights.

As explained in an earlier chapter, political power can be an influencing factor in how various communities are treated by governmental bureaucracies. People who vote and are part of the legislative process have a much better chance of acquiring resources for themselves and their communities, as well as influencing the policies that impact their lives. As a former legislator, I know that two of the first things some elected officials do when they receive mail from people is determine whether the writers live in their district and if they are registered to vote. If the answer to both questions is yes, these politicians become much more interested in what these people have to say. In a democracy, having and using the ability to vote, as well as continuing to participate in the political and legislative processes between elections, is an asset that can change the lives of individuals and communities.

Being confronted with all or just some of these collateral consequences of drug felonies just about guarantees marginalized status within society for most of the black women who were incarcerated for these relatively small amounts of crack cocaine. The disenfranchisement of black women has been consistent in the United States from the time they were introduced here as slaves. Even when black women do not have criminal records, as a group they occupy the lower levels of professional, income, employment, political, and power ladders. Simply being a black woman in America has been correlated with challenges that can be attributed to their dual roles as women and black people. The disenfranchisement goes beyond the woman herself and impacts the opportunities and quality of life available to her children, her family, and her community. The imprisonment of black women with no prior records, who were convicted for offenses that involved amounts of crack cocaine that are negligible as compared to powdered cocaine, perpetuated the marginalization of these women, as well as that of their families and communities. Is this justice? I think not.

Are the Federal Drug Laws Regarding Crack Cocaine Inherently Racist?

Without question, black women are represented disproportionately among females who are convicted and incarcerated for drug offenses that involve crack cocaine. This disproportionality is partially explained by the disparity contained within the drug laws requiring application of the 100:1 ratio of powdered cocaine to crack cocaine. The laws promulgate the incarceration of offenders involved with crack cocaine by enabling relatively small amounts of the drug to trigger the mandatory minimum sentencing, as compared to one hundred times those same amounts of powdered cocaine that are needed to institute the same penalties. Additionally, for the purpose of determining if threshold levels are attained for the imposition of mandatory minimum sentences, crack cocaine is weighed, including the weight of its filler (for example, sodium bicarbonate) in the total weight; however when powdered cocaine is weighed, these measurements take into account only the drug itself. Most crack cocaine is only 10 to 40 percent pure cocaine by weight.[329]

For a practical understanding of the 100:1 disparity, one should understand the differences in dosages produced by each form of cocaine as they relate to their threshold amounts. One gram of powdered cocaine may produce five to ten doses, and one gram of crack cocaine may produce two to ten doses. Therefore, five hundred grams of powdered cocaine (the threshold amount for powdered cocaine needed to trigger a mandatory minimum sentence of five years) produces 2,500 to 5,000 doses. In comparison, five grams of crack cocaine (the threshold amount for crack to trigger a mandatory minimum

---

329 Morgan and Zimmer, 1997.

sentence of five years) yields ten to fifty doses.[330] The disparities are quite pronounced.

The policing tactics employed to implement the law are also important factors in understanding the effect of the war on drugs on black women. Most of the efforts continue to focus on urban areas and consequently, concentrate on black and other minority groups. The results of the law and the policy tactics are that most of the people, including women, who are convicted and imprisoned for offenses involving crack cocaine, are black.

After extensive investigation, the United States Sentencing Commission determined that changes needed to be made to the laws requiring the mandatory minimum sentences for drug offenses that involved relatively small amounts of crack cocaine. In 1995, 1997, and 2002, the Commission recommended to Congress and President Clinton that there was no valid reason for the disparity existing between powdered cocaine and crack cocaine and that the amounts specified in the legislation should be adjusted to more realistically reflect the stated targets: mid-level dealers and people occupying higher levels in the drug hierarchy, as opposed to users and low-level dealers. Their recommendations were rejected, thus continuing the war on drugs into its second and third decades. Based upon Chambliss[331] and Scheingold's [332] explanations of the roles of the media, politics, self-serving agendas, and the public's (vicarious) fear of victimization, it is understandable why Congress and the president rejected the USSC's recommendation in 1995 and continued the policies that had so negatively impacted the black community. Chambliss's theory of law, order, and power, together with Scheingold's explanation of the cultural politicization of crime, would support the proposition that people who are elected to office, particularly politicians, may be more interested in attaining and remaining in office than in making decisions based on the apparent facts.[333] As a result, they will be less likely to vote to repeal legislation that satisfies the public's perception of crime control. This is particularly true when the victims, in this case black women and men, are politically powerless (many lose their voting rights when convicted of felonies) and are therefore unable to exert the same political pressure as middle-class voters who continue to enjoy and exercise their political strength. Law enforcement agencies that employ tactics that focus on open-air markets in urban areas, as opposed to drug purchasers in automobiles with license plates registered to owners of private homes in suburbia, have no incentive to change their practices.

330 USSC, 2002 Commission Report; USSC, May 2007.
331 Chambliss, 1969, 1971, 1995.
332 Scheingold, 1984.
333 My definition of *politicians*, as articulated above, is different than that of *elected officials* who make policy decisions based upon the information they have and what they feel is best for society, and not for their personal interest in reelection.

The more arrests that are made with the least political resistance, the more successful law enforcement efforts appear to be.

The disparate treatment of crack cocaine as compared to other drugs, particularly powdered cocaine, is closely related to the disproportionate representation of black females among women incarcerated for drug offenses by the federal government. Whether or not this differential impact is intentional is irrelevant for policy considerations. Laws that have a disparate impact on one segment of society are automatically suspect. As indicated by Gay McDougal of the United Nations Committee on the Elimination of Racial Discrimination, even if unintentional, when disparate impact is found, it must be dealt with.[334]

The United States Sentencing Commission followed in kind with the following statement:

> Sentencing rules that are needed to achieve the purposes of sentencing are fair, even if they adversely affect some groups more than others. But if a sentencing rule has a significant adverse impact and there is insufficient evidence that the rule is needed to achieve a statutory purpose of sentencing, then the rule might be considered unfair toward the affected groups.[335]

What must be queried now is whether the disparity inherent in both the mandatory minimum provisions for sentencing applied to crack cocaine offenses and the application of the drug law initiatives regarding crack cocaine that are related to the imprisonment of black females are worth the costs to individuals, communities, and society as a whole. The displacement of black women—from mainstream society to prison and then back to the community after five or ten years of imprisonment—comes at an exorbitant cost to all members of society. Is this justice?

Policy Issues

The purpose of this research is not to debate if the war on drugs is predominately a war against black females, black males, or women in general. The goal of the research is to better understand the impact of the legislative initiatives underlying the war on drugs on the incarceration of women in general, and on black women specifically. If the analyses indicate that the differential impact on black women or other demographic groups is not related to, and outweighed by, a reduction in drug use or violent crimes, then these

---

334 CNN, *Face to Face*, Sunday, 1/09/2000.
335 USSC, November, 2004, 114.

policies may be deemed to be suspect and their continued existence must be questioned.

Although the war on drugs began more than two decades ago and most media attention on the subject has diminished, the initiatives of the war are still in effect and being enforced. Black women have suffered greatly from the drug policies that focus on: (a) imprisoning people who are involved in drug offenses with relatively small amounts of crack cocaine and (b) the law enforcement strategies of policing that concentrate on inner cities. The ADAAs of 1986 and 1988 were developed during times of intense focus by the media to stimulate and maintain the public's attention on the use of crack cocaine with little or no research on the effects of crack cocaine and with the attachment of campaigning politicians to these policies, which then had popular appeal. This study, using current data, shows that the war on drugs continues to impact black women who are convicted of drug offenses disproportionately.

Black women who are convicted of drug offenses that involve crack cocaine continue to be easy targets for the war on drugs. Initially, they were portrayed by the media as worthy of punishment because of their lifestyles. They lacked the political strength to fight against the enactment or modification of the legislative initiatives and laws that imprisoned them. There was a strong correlation between the increase in the imprisonment of black women due to the implementation of the war on drugs with its mandatory minimum sentencing laws, focus on first-time offenders, and criminalization of crack cocaine abusers. This study substantiates the relationship between these factors and the current imprisonment of black women in the federal system.

The drug policies that required mandatory minimum sentences for various types of drugs brought more women, particularly black, Hispanic, and white women, into the criminal justice system and were, at the very least, related to the tremendous increase in the number of incarcerated women in the United States. Considering that women have historically been major consumers and abusers of drugs, one can easily understand how policies that include the imprisonment of drug abusers would cause more women to become part of the criminal justice system. Surveys of populations of women prisoners over the years have consistently indicated that most imprisoned women committed the offenses for which they were incarcerated either to obtain drugs or to secure money to buy drugs. These studies have also substantiated the prevalence of the use of hard drugs on an ongoing basis by female arrestees and inmates. However, most of these women did not commit violent offenses.

Judge Gladys Kessler of the National Association of Women Judges testified before the Senate Judiciary Committee that the majority of women who are imprisoned represent the "lowest, most easily arrested rung of the drug crime business." Kessler further stated that these female offenders are "ideal candidates for community placement."[336] Unfortunately, in 1996, drug policies did not allow for such placements. By 2006, there was great movement by several individuals and organizations to provide for alternatives to policies that instituted widespread incarceration for low-level drug offenders, including drug courts, more grounds for downward departures, and challenges to the mandatory nature of the sentencing guidelines.

More than twenty years after the beginning the war on drugs, there are two questions that must be answered:

1. Are the current drug policies meeting their goals of reduced use and abuse of drugs?

2. Are the effects of the policies worth the results?

Although mandatory minimum sentencing has been the mainstay of the drug laws for the federal and many state governments, many practitioners and researchers agree that behaviors constituting drug law violations are uniquely insensitive to the deterrent effects of sanctions.

> The proliferation of mandatory penalties for drug crimes in the 1980s did not demonstrably reduce drug trafficking (Reuter and Kleiman 1986, table 5; Moore 1990, figure 1).... There is little basis for believing that mandatory penalties have any significant effects on rates of serious crime. The list of problems with any mandatory penalties, however, only begins with their crime-prevention ineffectiveness. They do great harm to the integrity of case processing and sentencing and often result in the imposition of manifestly unjust punishments (Tonry, 1995: 141–142).[337]

This position is difficult to refute, particularly when one considers the increasing number of people who continue to be incarcerated for drug offenses and the cost of constructing prisons to house them.[338] If the policies were effective, the number of drug offenders would decline because of the laws. Instead, the only major impact of the policies has been on the growth of the

---

336 Flanders, 1994.

337 Tonry, 1995, 141–142.

338 Although prisons located in economically depressed areas are advantageous (i.e., jobs and services) to the area and politically beneficial to the politicians who sponsor them, the cost to taxpayers is prohibitive at twenty-five to thirty thousand dollars per inmate per year.

prison population, particularly for black women convicted of crack cocaine offenses and Hispanic women convicted for offenses involving marijuana and powdered cocaine.

The negative impact of these drug policies on families and communities is also without question. Most incarcerated women have children.[339] The separation of a mother from her child has far-reaching effects. Current research indicates that the incarceration of a mother may cause more harm to a child than the incarceration of the child's father.[340] When a mother is incarcerated, the effects on her child are similar to the grief and loss experienced upon the death of a parent.[341] Such emotional trauma can lead to behaviors from the children that bring them into the juvenile justice system. Also, the children of mothers who are incarcerated are often displaced from their living situations and may be required to live with grandparents or transferred to already overburdened foster care systems. Many states have also implemented laws that terminate the parental rights of parents who have little or no contact with their children after a specified number of months. In 1997, the federal government enacted the Adoption and Safe Families Act (ASFA). ASFA allows for the termination of parental rights when a child has lived in foster care for the last fifteen of twenty-two months. Considering that 84 percent of parents incarcerated in federal prisons are more than one hundred miles away from their hometowns, 42 percent are incarcerated more than five hundred miles away, and women convicted of crack offenses are getting mandatory minimum sentences of five and ten years, it is extremely difficult for children and incarcerated mothers to stay in contact. In fact, the frequency of contact between children and their federally incarcerated parents decreased by 28.6 percent between 1997 and 2004. In 2004, only 17 percent of the parents reported having at least one contact of any kind per month with their children. In 1996, 8.8 percent reported that they never had contact of any kind with their children, which was a 17.3 percent increase since 1997.[342]

A complex tangle of issues and effects must be considered when people, particularly women, are incarcerated because of policies that were developed purely for political gain in an atmosphere of public hysteria created by the media. Subsequent research indicates that much of the basis of the hype promulgated by the media has not materialized:

---

339   Glick and Neto, 1977; BJS, 1994; The Punitiveness Report. Hit Hard: The Growth in the Growth in the Imprisonment of Women, 1977–2004, Institute on Women and Criminal Justice.

340   Sentencing Project (2009). Incarcerated Parents and Their Children, 1991–2007, February 2009.

341   Bloom and Steinhart, 1993.

342   Sentencing Project, 2009. Table 6, p. 7.

- Addiction to crack cocaine is not increasing, and people addicted to crack are not more violent than other drug abusers.[343]

- Crack cocaine has not been proven to be more addictive than powdered cocaine.[344] Once cocaine of any form reaches the brain, the same physiological and psychotropic effects occur.[345]

- Babies born to women who used crack cocaine during their pregnancies are not physically dependent on the drug and do not experience symptoms of drug withdrawal.[346] The negative effects are identical to those experienced by babies exposed prenatally to powdered cocaine.[347] (Additionally, research indicates that one cannot determine the difference in effects between crack and powdered cocaine because the substances are indistinguishable once ingested; many findings of effects are correlated with the prenatal exposure of children to tobacco, marijuana, alcohol, and the quality of the child's environment.[348])

What is true is that the war on drugs in the United States continues to swell the prisons with women who have been convicted of possession and trafficking—low-level drug offenses. What is also true is that most of these women have drug problems and have never received treatment. It would be more cost effective—both in monetary and social currency—to treat addicted women outside of costly prison walls that separate mothers from children, women from productive futures, and taxpayers from other services.

Policy Changes

I personally observed as a legislator that it is often very difficult to convince legislators to amend or abolish criminal laws because of their fear of being labeled "soft on crime" by the public and political rivals. This is particularly true when the people who advocate for change are not their constituents or people they judge as not having very much political clout. This appeared to be operative in the attempts to change the 100:1 powdered cocaine

---

343 Webb and Brown, 1998; Morgan and Zimmer, 1997.

344 Morgan and Zimmer, 1997; USSC, May, 2007.

345 Written Statement by Nora D. Volkow, M.D., Director, National Institute on Drug Abuse (NIDA), to the United States Sentencing Commission, regarding Cocaine Sentencing Policy, at 1. As reported in USSC, May 2007, p.64.

346 Morgan and Zimmer, 1997.

347 USSC, May 2007, p.62.

348 Deborah A. Frank, et al., Growth, Development, and Behavior in Early Childhood Following Prenatal Cocaine Exposure: A Systematic Review, 285 *Journal of the American Medical Association* 1613–1625 (2001).

ratios contained in the Anti-Drug Abuse Acts of 1986 and 1989 during the 1980s and 1990s. It is also possible that some of the legislators felt that the research had yet to support the need for change. However, particularly since 1996, major attempts have been made to modify the law, and most of the proposals and support for change have come from people and entities with political power. These advocates for change have included the United States Sentencing Commission; federal judges and judicial organizations; the Federal Public and Community Defenders; the American Bar Association; the National Association of Criminal Defense Lawyers; several members of the medical, scientific, and treatment communities; academics; Families Against Mandatory Minimums; the NAACP; and the Sentencing Project, to name a few.[349] The cumulative political power brought to bear by their banding together may have—probably did—provide what was needed for some successful policy changes from any number of different arenas. Most of these initiatives have focused on: (a) reducing the 100:1 ratio of powdered to crack cocaine, (b) removing the mandatory sentencing requirements attached to the laws, or (c) changing the sentencing guidelines attached to the sentences imposed on people convicted of crack cocaine offenses.

Some of the major initiatives that have been successful in addressing the landscape of the cocaine sentencing disparity are discussed below.

— *United States v. Booker, 543 U.S. 220 (2005)*

In this case, the Supreme Court ruled that the sentencing guidelines were not mandatory. This decision allowed judges to use more discretion in sentencing offenders, including drug offenders. The result of this ruling has been that some district courts do attempt to mitigate the 100:1 powdered to crack cocaine disparity by not following the sentencing guidelines. The district courts' rulings have not been consistent and are reviewable by courts of appeals on the subjective basis of "reasonableness." The questions remained as to whether and how the district courts should consider the cocaine sentencing disparity in their sentencing of defendants convicted of crack offenses.[350]

United States Sentencing Commission

The United States Sentencing Commission exercised its authority and submitted amendments to Congress in 2007 that would change the federal sentencing guidelines. One of these amendments specifically changed the drug quantity thresholds thus changing the sentencing ranges for crack cocaine. The guidelines basically adjusted downward by two levels for crack cocaine

---

349 USSC, May 2007, Report to Congress Cocaine and Federal Sentencing Policy (Washington, DC), Appendices B and C.

350 USSC, May 2007, p.115.

offenses for quantities above and below the mandatory minimum threshold amounts. The amendment became effective on November 1, 2007, and the Commission voted to apply the amendments retroactively to March 3, 2008. Consequently, by 2009, approximately twelve thousand people who were incarcerated for crack cocaine offenses had been released.[351] The Commission clearly indicated that, for true change to occur, Congress would need to change the ADAAs.

— Proposed Legislation

There is an inherent responsibility for all policymakers to be aware of the effects of their initiatives; this includes determining if the effects of the implemented policies impact differentially upon certain groups of the population. By 2006, more federal legislators began to question the efficacy of the differential treatment of powdered and crack cocaine offenders. Although not successful to date, some members of Congress introduced bills to change the 100:1 ratio between powdered and crack cocaine. Although most bills urged that the ratios be reduced but that a disparity remain, there were two companion bills introduced that would completely eliminate the disparity between powdered and crack cocaine. The Senate version of the bill, entitled Drug Sentencing Reform and Kingpin Trafficking Act of 2007 (S. 1711), was introduced by then Senator Joseph Biden. The companion bill, H.R. 4545, was introduced by Congresswoman Sheila Jackson-Lee. This legislation also included a treatment provision. The bill did not pass during the 2007–2008 session. In 2009, H.R. 3245, a bill entitled Fairness in Cocaine Sentencing Act of 2009, was introduced by Congressman Robert Scott. The purpose of the bill was to eliminate the increased penalties for cocaine offenses involving crack cocaine as compared to powdered cocaine. At the time of the writing of this book, the legislation is still in committee.

— Executive Branch

In 2008, Barack Obama was elected to the presidency of the United States. Although he faced more challenges than any other president in United States history—a failing economy, two wars, environmental issues, and a health care system in need of revamping—President Obama included in his goals his intention to address the disparities between powdered and crack cocaine. This was the first time in history that a president had done so. At the time of the writing of this book, President Obama is only a year past assuming

---

351   USSC, February 2009. United States Sentencing Commission's Preliminary Crack Cocaine Restructuring Data Report, February 2009 data.

office. It is too soon to know if the disparity will be addressed, but it is possible that a window of opportunity exists now more than ever to effectuate such change.

— *Future Possibilities*

The second decade of the twenty-first century presents an opportunity to change the elements of the Anti-Drug Abuse Acts of 1986 and 1988 that require disparity between the responses to drug offenses involving powdered and crack cocaine. Fiscal matters are an important part of public policy. Not only are there more people and entities willing to move for such change, and a president and vice president who support removal of the disparities, but the financial woes of the United States and the world economies provide an additional incentive for change. More people who thought they were not affected by these laws will better understand how all taxpayers pay the costs of incarceration, whether they pertain to building and maintaining prisons or imprisoning women for five, ten, or twenty years and more, as well as the costs associated with the collateral consequences of mothers, daughters, family members, and neighbors leaving their homes and communities. The economic challenges faced by the United States mandate a new review of the feasibility and economic costs and benefits of incarcerating low-level crack cocaine offenders.

In conducting this feasibility study, it is clear that in addition to evaluating social costs, we must consider whether it is fiscally responsible to incarcerate a person for five or ten years because of the sentencing disparity between powdered and crack cocaine. This cost analysis must include the financial costs to the taxpayers for meeting the needs of children whose mothers are incarcerated for low-level amounts of crack cocaine for several years, as well as the resources required to meet the reentry needs of women after so many years of incarceration and the resulting barriers presented by felony drug convictions. These costs must be compared to alternative approaches such as community placements, mental health counseling, and residential drug treatment.

Conclusions

This policy analysis substantiates the need to revisit and revise the mandatory minimum sentencing provisions that require the incarceration of people who are convicted of drug offenses that involve less than five hundred grams of crack cocaine. This study shows that these laws have a major impact on black women who are brought into the federal system for such offenses. If a woman is convicted in the federal system of an offense that involves crack cocaine, she is most likely to be black and to have dependent children. These black women, with little or no prior records, involved in small amounts of drugs, will continue to be incarcerated with prison terms that are far in excess of those they would have received for handling the drug in its elemental, more potent form (powdered cocaine) unless the laws themselves—the Anti-Drug Abuse Acts of 1986 and 1988, with their focus on very low levels of crack cocaine—are changed. The attempts to mitigate the harshness of the laws by changing the applicable sentencing guidelines, and through various types of downward departures and role adjustments, have had positive—but minimal—effects on the sentences these women receive.

What can be done to change this situation? These research findings indicate that it is not simply the behavior of the black females nor racism in the attitudes and behavior of decision makers in the criminal justice system (as discovered by other researchers) that severely impact the likelihood of black women being incarcerated for long periods of time for drug offenses involving crack cocaine. The laws must be amended to effectuate change in the impact of the war on drugs on black females. To appropriately address the issue, the threshold amounts that trigger the mandatory minimum sentences for offenses involving crack cocaine should be changed to bring them more in line with those applicable to offenses involving powdered cocaine. Research now exists that supports the need and rationale for these changes. Furthermore, the method of weighing crack cocaine—by including the non-drug fillers such as sodium bicarbonate—should be changed. Crack should be weighed in the same manner as powdered cocaine; only the drug should be included in the weight that determines if the threshold has been met for mandatory minimum sentencing. Changes have taken place since 1996, but the law remains the same.

To implement an amendment to the Anti-Drug Abuse Acts of 1986 and 1988, the public must be made aware of the inequities of the 100:1 ratio for crack cocaine and powdered cocaine. Based upon my personal experience as a state legislator, I understand that it is difficult to get people involved in government and law when they don't feel that they are directly impacted by the policies. Elected officials often don't want to undertake legislation that will repeal or significantly lessen the draconian effects on some crime bills because of their fear of being portrayed as "soft on crime" by potential challengers in future elections. However, I also know that an informed public can support and direct their legislators to sponsor and support—or at least not jeopardize—the passage of public policies that reframe laws that needlessly and ineffectively target the wrong people. Any change to federal drug policies involving crack cocaine will require the continued education of the public and their elected representatives. In addition to the financial and social costs that must be paid if the laws are allowed to remain as they are, there is an ethical responsibility for change to be made. Our current state of knowledge about crack cocaine and its effects on people (including babies) and crime is much greater now, more than twenty years after the enactment of the Anti-Drug Abuse Acts of 1986 and 1988, and it does not support the policies contained therein. Just as important, we have information about the impacts of the Anti-Drug Abuse Acts of 1986 and 1988, on black women, men, families, communities, and taxpayers, and they make the policies suspect.

Although the war on drugs may not have been intended to target black women, it was racially motivated by media portrayals of black people as the most prevalent users of crack cocaine. Because of the dual status of black females and the focus of the laws on crack cocaine, it was inevitable that black women would fall victim to the legislation and be pulled into the prison system for little or no involvement or conspiracy. Most importantly, if in arguendo, the results were not initially predicted or intended to impact black women so harshly, based upon what we know now, the continuation of the effect of the disparate treatment of crack cocaine and powdered cocaine on the imprisonment of black women and black men, becomes intentional, as do the costs to the affected individuals, children, and communities.

Where is the justice in allowing these laws to continue to imprison so many people for so little involvement? Where is the justice in keeping so many low-level drug offenders incarcerated for so long for such minimal participation in drug crimes? I am hopeful that after decades of injustice a window of opportunity will open to allow the necessary research, political power, and civic involvement to come together to first do away with the disparity within the law between crack cocaine and powdered cocaine by making the threshold amounts for incarceration and sentencing equal for the two forms of cocaine; second, revisit the appropriateness of mandatory minimum sentencing for any offenses; third, apply any changes to the drug policies for crack cocaine retroactively so that the thousands of women and men who are serving extraordinary sentences that are now shown to be unfounded based on the research, on the stated intent of the acts to penalize drug kings, and on social justice, can also experience justice; and fourth, cause voters and politicians to commit to requiring that all legislation and policies, drug-related or not, be supported by evidence and research. Emotion and media hype alone can lead to policies that intentionally or unintentionally target groups of people who do not match the stated purpose of laws, and the devastating impact that the war on drugs has had on black women and men will last for decades to come.

Allowing the continuation of the drug policies that apply mandatory minimum sentences to small quantities of crack cocaine and that imprison low-level drug offenders, including black women who have little or no prior criminal records, for unbelievably long sentences, as well as the 100:1 disparity applied to powdered cocaine and crack cocaine, is unjust.

───── APPENDIX A ─────
Variables

Demographic Group

Demographic group represents the racial or ethnic group with which the individual woman in the case is identified. In this study, this variable has three categories: black women, Hispanic women, and white women. These three groups were included in the study because of their substantial presence in the population of women who are incarcerated in the federal system. Although other racial/ethnic groups of women are incarcerated in the federal system (Native American, Asian, Pacific Islander, and Alaskan/Inuit women), their numbers are relatively small in comparison to black, white, and Hispanic females. This variable is used to segment the sample into racial/ethnic groups. It is measured at the nominal level.

Criminal History

Criminal history is included in this research because of its importance in decisions that affect sentencing and detention. Mann[352] indicated that she was unable to control for the prior records of the subjects in her study. By including the variable for criminal history, this research does control for prior record.

Criminal history, or prior record, is a legal variable because it is both appropriate and expected that a person's prior record will be considered when decisions regarding the type of sentence and amount of time a defendant must serve under supervision both prior to and after the adjudication of her or his

---

352 Mann, 1995.

case are rendered. A judge is usually required to consider the prior record of a convicted person when determining the extent and length of time the subject will be remanded to supervision under the criminal justice system. In cases where mandatory minimum sentences are not applicable, an offender with a minimal or no prior record often receives a less stringent sentence than a person under similar circumstances who has an extensive or serious record.

The criminal history variable in this study is operationalized in two ways. One is as an ordinal level variable that represents the final criminal history category as determined by the judge and provided by the USSC. There are six categories of criminal history to which a defendant can be assigned. The second method of operationalization consists of a variable that reflects the total number of criminal history points awarded to the defendant in the case and is an interval level variable. The designation represents the total number of points assigned by the judge based upon the defendant's criminal history. The total number of points assigned for the criminal history category is calculated using the guidelines promulgated by the United States Sentencing Commission and that are contained in United States Sentencing Commission Section 4A1.1, which follows:

Criminal History Category:

The total points derived from items (a) through (f) determine the category of criminal in the Sentencing Table.

(a) Add 3 points for each prior sentence of imprisonment that exceeds one year and one month.

(b) Add 2 points for each prior sentence of imprisonment of at least sixty days not counted in (a).

(c) Add 1 point for each prior sentence not counted in (a) or (b), up to 4 points for this item.

(d) Add 2 points if the defendant committed the instant offense while under any sentence of the criminal justice system, including probation, parole, supervised release, imprisonment, work release, or escape status.

(e) Add 2 points if the defendant committed the instant offense less than two years after release from imprisonment on a sentence counted under (a) or (b) or while in imprisonment or escape status on such a sentence. If 2 points are added for item (d), add only 1 point for this item.

(f) Add 1 point for each prior sentence resulting from a conviction of a crime of violence that did not receive any points under (a), (b), or (c) above, because such sentence was considered related to another sentence resulting from a conviction of a crime of violence, to a total of 3 points for this item. *Provided*, that this item does not apply where the sentences considered related because the offenses occurred on the same occasion.

Under mandatory minimum sentencing schemes, a person's criminal history is generally not a factor that can mitigate or shorten the length of sentence, although it may be used to enhance or lengthen the time of incarceration.

— Drug Type

Drug type is included in the analyses in order to begin the investigation of the relationship between each group of women with crack cocaine and other types of drugs. Drug type is operationalized by the use of three variables: (a) type of drug (for the descriptive analyses), (b) crack cocaine as compared to drugs other than crack cocaine, and (c) crack cocaine as compared to powdered cocaine. The type of drug variable used in the analyses consists of six categories. The type of drugs include: (1) cocaine; (2) crack; (3) heroin; (4) marijuana; (5) all methamphetamines; and (6) other (which includes hashish, LSD, PCP, ICE, Ecstasy, steroids, amphetamines, dilaudid, opium, other, nonspecific, methcathinone). The drugs listed in category six are listed together because all have low levels of frequency within the sample. The drug type variables that compare crack cocaine to all other drugs or to powdered cocaine, are dummy variables and are also used.

— Drug Mandatory Minimum Sentence

Drug mandatory minimum sentence is a nominal level variable that reflects if a mandatory minimum sentence for drugs is applied. There are two categories for this variable: 0 indicates that no statutory drug mandatory minimum was applied, and 1 indicates a statutory drug mandatory minimum was applied. The drug mandatory minimum variable combined with drug type, specifically crack cocaine, is used to represent the construct "war on drugs."

— *Drug Amount in Grams*

The variable drug amount in grams is used to test the influence of the amount of drugs involved in the offense on the decision to incarcerate and the length of prison sentence imposed. This is an interval-level variable that reflects the actual amount of the drug in grams.

The mandatory minimum sentences associated with crack cocaine offenses prescribe the imposition of imprisonment for small amounts of the drug.

— *Departure from Mandatory Minimum Sentencing*

As discussed in chapter four, in 1986, Congress mandated that the United States Sentencing Commission provide statutory incentives for the cooperation of defendants who assist in the investigation and prosecution of other persons for other crimes. The USSC established a guideline commonly referred to as a 5K1.1 motion. The 5K1.1 motion allows a prosecutor to motion the court for a downward departure of sentence below the established guidelines or mandatory sentencing established for the offense. The magnitude of the departure is within the discretion of the judge to impose. For several years, this was the only departure authorized by statute.[353] Subsequent to 1996, several other types of downward departures have been allowed.[354] These are included in the analyses of the 2006 data to determine what, if any, affect they had on the decision to incarcerate or the length of prison sentence.

A variable labeled downward departure is included in the analyses. The variable is a dichotomous dummy variable for which 0 means no downward departure and 1 indicates a downward departure is applied. In some instances the reason for the departure is not provided by the judge; however, these cases are coded as downward departures in this study.

The downward departure variable is used in both the descriptive and multivariate analyses. It is predicted that the variable will not be significant for black women who were convicted of drug offenses involving crack cocaine in 1996, but is expected to prove to have been significant in 2006 because of the change in attitude about the punitive effect of mandatory minimum sentencing on low-level drug offenders.

— *Interaction between Drug Mandatory Minimum and Drug Type*

Some of the hypotheses include this variable, which represents the effect of the imposition of a mandatory minimum sentence for a drug offense that involves crack cocaine. It is a dummy variable (nominal) and has two

---

353 Maxfield and Kramer, 1998.
354 See chapter four for a more detailed discussion of departures.

categories: 0, for when a drug mandatory minimum is not imposed and/or crack is not the primary drug involved, and 1, for when a drug mandatory minimum is imposed for a drug offense that involves crack cocaine. Because of the expected association between black females in the federal system and crack cocaine, and because relatively small amounts of crack cocaine trigger the mandatory minimum sentences for a drug offense, it is hypothesized that this variable will be significant for black females in predicting both if prison sentences were imposed and the length of prison sentences ordered. It is not predicted that this interaction will significantly affect the decision to incarcerate or the length of prison sentences imposed for white or Hispanic women because it is not expected that a significant number of either group will be shown to have been convicted of crack cocaine offenses.

— *Imposition of Mandatory Minimum Sentences of Zero, Five, or Ten Years*

The variables that represent the imposition of a sentence of zero, five, or ten years are dichotomous dependent variables. Dichotomous variables that represent the likelihood of receiving a sentence for five years or a sentence for ten years are analyzed using logistic regression. Although this variable may be viewed as an ordinal-level variable, logistic regression is used to analyze the odds of the subjects' being in each of the three categories as opposed to calculating the odds of their receiving one sentence or a lesser sentence, which is often the result in methods that focus on the ordinal nature of a variable.[355]

These dependent variables are included because, although a mandatory minimum sentence may be required by statute, in some instances the judge does not apply it. Although the only accepted reason by statute for such an action was a downward departure for substantial assistance, this was not the case in 2006, as additional statutory bases were in effect by that time for not ordering the required mandatory minimum sentence. Additionally, the effects of several extralegal variables are also tested.

— *Prison In/Out*

The variable prison in/out is a dependent variable. It is incorporated in the study to reflect the decision to incarcerate or not to incarcerate. The variable is measured at the nominal level and is treated as a dummy variable. There are two categories for prison in/out: 0, which indicates an individual did not receive a prison sentence, and 1, indicating that a woman did receive a prison sentence.

---

355 DeMaris, 1992.

— *Total Amount of Prison Time Ordered*

This dependent variable is operationalized as the total number of months sentenced to prison. It is measured at the interval level and reflects either the actual number of months imposed by the judge, or if the sentence is more than 990 months, life, or the death penalty, the value 990 is used. This variable is also the basis of the natural log of the length of prison sentence.

— *Log of Length of Prison Sentence*

This variable is used in the multivariate analyses to reflect the natural log of the number of months a woman convicted of a drug offense is sentenced to prison. This variable is measured at the interval level and is a dependent variable. The natural log of the total number of months sentenced to prison is taken to achieve linearity.[356] The analyses indicating the log of prison do not include cases in which there was no imprisonment.[357]

---

356 Norusis, 1993.
357 Weisburd, Wheeler, Waring, and Bode, 1991.

APPENDIX B

Descriptive Statistics of Variables
for Full Sample

B.1: Descriptive Statistics of Variables for Full Sample, 1996

	N Statistic	Minimum Statistic	Maximum Statistic	Mean Statistic	Std. Deviation Statistic	Variance Statistic	Skew Statistic	Std. Error	Kurtosis Statistic	Std. Error
Demographic group	2130	1	3	1.99	.82	.676	.014	.053	-1.521	.106
Downward departure	2055	0	1	.46	.50	.249	.153	.054	-1.978	.108
Statutory drug min	2123	0	1	.56	.50	.247	-.233	.053	-1.948	.106
No mandatory minimum imposed	2130	0	1	.44	.50	.247	.238	.053	-1.945	.106
Five years	2130	0	1	.26	.44	.194	1.072	.053	-.851	.106
Ten years	2130	0	1	.27	.45	.198	1.024	.053	-.953	.106
Drug: crack cocaine	2129	0	1	.23	.42	.177	1.289	.053	-.338	.106
Mand min* crack cocaine	2128	0	1	.16	.37	.136	1.830	.053	1.350	.106
Offense: drug distribution/manufacturing	2130	0	1	.72	.45	.202	-.974	.053	-1.052	.106
Offense: simple possession	2130	0	1	5.82E-02	.23	5.485E-02	3.776	.053	12.271	.106
Offense: forgery or fraud for drugs	2130	0	1	3.76E-03	6.12E-02	3.744E-03	16.237	.053	261.871	.106
Offense: other drug offenses	2130	0	0	.00	.00	.000	.	.	.	.
Offense: drug importation/exportation	2130	0	1	.15	.36	.126	1.985	.053	1.943	.106
Offense: distribution near school	2130	0	1	2.82E-03	5.30E-02	2.810E-03	18.775	.053	350.829	.106
Offense: distribution employ person under twenty-one	2130	0	1	4.69E-04	2.17E-02	4.695E-04	46.152	.053	2130.000	.106
Offense: distribution/manufacturing - conspiracy	2130	0	1	9.39E-04	3.06E-02	9.385E-04	32.611	.053	1062.496	.106
Offense: continuing criminal enterprise	2130	0	1	1.41E-03	3.75E-02	1.407E-03	26.608	.053	706.662	.106
Offense: communication facility	2130	0	1	4.23E-02	.20	4.049E-02	4.554	.053	18.758	.106
Offense: establish/rent drug establishment	2130	0	1	2.11E-02	.14	2.069E-02	6.665	.053	42.457	.106

Offense: distribution or possession of listed chemicals	2130	0	1	2.35E-03	4.84E-02	2.343E-03	20.582	.053	421.995	.106
Log of "totprison"	1732	0	7	3.58	1.03	1.065	-.346	.059	1.209	.118
Type of drug offense	2130	1	11	2.15	2.59	6.698	2.290	.053	3.693	.106
Crack vs. powdered cocaine	1052	0	1	.46	.50	.249	.145	.075	-1.983	.151
Prison in/out	2116	0	1	.82	.39	.149	-1.654	.053	.737	.106
Role adjustment-highest	2121	0	1	.39	.49	.237	.470	.053	-1.781	.106
Number of criminal history points	2119	0	27	1.42	2.94	8.621	3.499	.053	16.505	.106
Num total months imprisonment ordered	2116	0	996	49.66	92.73	8598.770	7.393	.053	69.600	.106
Drug amount in grams	1791	.0000	4535999999.8639	12900055.910470	239482071.328481	57351662487779800.000	18.841	.058	353.632	.116
Drug amount in grams (n)	2130	.0000	4535999999.8639	10849411.454626	219640188.047371	48241812205484600.000	20.558	.053	421.326	.106
Final criminal history category	1996	1	6	1.52	1.10	1.206	2.536	.055	6.323	.110
Valid N (listwise)	737									

Source: ICPSR 9317, FY 1996.

B.2: Descriptive Statistics of Variables for Full Sample, 2006

Descriptive Statistics										
							Skewness		Kurtosis	
	N Statistic	Minimum Statistic	Maximum Statistic	Mean Statistic	Std. Deviation Statistic	Variance Statistic	Statistic	Std. Error	Statistic	Std. Error
RaceEth	3050	1.00	3.00	1.9767	.89957	.809	.046	.044	-1.763	.089
Drug_type	2992	1.00	6.00	3.4422	1.63545	2.675	-.199	.045	-1.263	.089
Receiv_prison	3050	.00	1.00	.8269	.37841	.143	-1.729	.044	.989	.089
Prior_rec	3017	1.00	6.00	1.6550	1.18397	1.402	1.968	.045	3.374	.089
Mand_min_drug	3050	.0	1.0	.546	.4979	.248	-.186	.044	-1.967	.089
Drugmin	3050	0	9996	65.61	364.240	132670.830	26.602	.044	723.225	.089
Prisdum	3041	0	1	.89	.310	.096	-2.535	.044	4.429	.089
Crack_no_crack	3050	.00	1.00	.1570	.36391	.132	1.886	.044	1.558	.089
Drg_man_min_0	3012	.00	1.00	.4595	.49844	.248	.163	.045	-1.975	.089
Drg_man_min_5	3050	.00	1.00	.2230	.41629	.173	1.332	.044	-.226	.089
Drg_man_min_10	3050	.00	1.00	.2967	.45689	.209	.890	.044	-1.208	.089
Roladj1	3014	0	1	.37	.484	.234	.527	.045	-1.723	.089
Downward_departure	3013	.000	1.000	.51875	.499731	.250	-.075	.045	-1.996	.089
Type_drug_off	3050	1.00	3.00	1.0872	.37502	.141	4.417	.044	18.607	.089
Drug_min_crack	3050	.00	1.00	.1066	.30860	.095	2.552	.044	4.513	.089
Powder_crack	1041	.00	1.00	.4601	.49865	.249	.160	.076	-1.978	.151
Grams	2207	1.00	9.00	7.3018	2.34695	5.508	-.935	.052	-.585	.104
Totprisn_recode	2513	1.00	9997.00	74.0163	445.50136	198471.458	22.008	.049	487.928	.098
Drug_trafficking	3050	.00	1.00	.9433	.23135	.054	-3.835	.044	12.713	.089
Drug_communication_facilities	3050	.00	1.00	.0262	.15984	.026	5.932	.044	33.208	.089
Drug_simple_possession	3050	.00	1.00	.0305	.17196	.030	5.464	.044	27.875	.089
Valid N (listwise)	0									

Source: ICPSR 20120, FY2006.

─────── APPENDIX C ───────

Descriptive Statistics of Black Women with No Prior Record Convicted of Offenses that Involved Less than Five Hundred Grams of Crack and Sentenced under Mandatory Minimum

C.1: Descriptive Statistics of Black Women with No Prior Record Convicted of Offenses that Involve Less than Five Hundred Grams of Crack and Sentenced under Mandatory Minimum, 1996

	N	MINIMUM	MAXIMUM	MEAN	STD. DEVIATION
Age of defendant at sentencing	93	19	58	31.61	9.66
Level of education completed	93	0	16	11.01	2.17
Number of dependants	93	0	9	1.87	1.82
Total number of criminal history points	93	0	1	.17	.38
Total number of months imprisoned	93	5	240	70.13	45.33
Total amount of drugs in grams	93	.0000	498.5700	136.176715	138.032854
Valid N	93				

Source: ICPSR 9317, FY1996, criminal history category=1.

C.2: Descriptive Statistics of Black Women with No Prior Record Convicted of Offenses that Involve Less than Five Hundred Grams of Crack and Sentenced under Mandatory Minimum, 2006

	N	MINIMUM	MAXIMUM	MEAN	STD. DEVIATION
Age of defendant at offense	62	20	55	31.31	8.85
*Level of education completed**	60 (2 missing)	1	5	3.20	1.29
Number of dependants	62	0	5	1.08	1.27
Total number of criminal history points	62	1.00	1.00	1.00	.000
Total number of months imprisoned	62	0	132	46.89	31.49
Total amount of drugs in grams	62	5.59	457.80	84.666	104.47

Source: ICPSR 20120, FY2006, criminal history category=1.

*1=Less than high school; 2=Some high school; 3=High school graduate or GED; 5=Some college

APPENDIX D

Descriptive Tables

Table D-1: Drug Convictions within and between Demographic Groups, 1996

Type of Drug	Black Women			Hispanic Women			White Women		
	Number convicted	Percent within group	Percent of all women drug offenders of this drug type	Number convicted	Percent within group	Percent of all women drug offenders of this drug type	Number convicted	Percent within group	Percent of all women drug offenders of this drug types
Powdered cocaine	219	30.1	38.8	209	30.3	37.1	136	19.1	24.1
Crack	370	50.8	75.8	44	6.4	9.0	74	10.4	15.2
Heroin	70	9.6	24.1	185	26.9	63.8	35	4.9	12.1
Marijuana	55	7.6	11.4	215	31.2	44.5	213	29.9	44.1
All methamphetamines	1	.1	.5	31	4.5	14.2	187	26.3	85.4
Other drugs	13	1.8	15.3	5	.7	5.9	67	9.4	78.8
Total	728	100	---	689	100	---	712	100	---

N = 2129, Chi-square=1000.58, p<.00001.

Table D.2: Drug Convictions within and between Demographic Groups, 2006

Type of drug	Black Women			Hispanic Women			White Women		
	Number convicted	Percent within group	Percent of all women drug offenders of this drug type	Number convicted	Percent within group	Percent of all women drug offenders of this drug type	Number convicted	Percent within group	Percent of all women drug offenders of this drug type
Powdered cocaine	156	24.0	25.7	327	26.1	53.8	125	9.3	20.6
Crack	306	47.0	59.1	47	3.8	9.1	165	12.2	31.9
Heroin	61	9.4	24.2	146	11.7	57.9	45	3.3	17.9
Marijuana	72	11.1	8.8	474	37.9	57.9	272	20.2	33.3
All methamphetamines	9	1.4	1.2	199	15.9	26.6	540	40.1	72.2
Other drugs	47	7.2	15.4	58	4.6	19.0	201	14.9	65.7
Total	651	100.0	20.0	1251	100.0	38.5	1348	100	41.5

N = 3250, Chi-square = 1253.8, p<.001.

Table D.3: Total Statutory Drug Minimum
Applicable in Months, 1996

Months	Frequency	Percent	Cum Percent
0	939	44.1	44.2
1	2	.1	44.3
12	10	.5	44.8
36	1	.0	44.8
60	562	26.4	71.3
120	580	27.2	98.6
180	4	.2	98.8
240	18	.8	99.7
Life imprisonment	7	.3	100.0
Missing	7	.3	
Total	**2130**	**100**	

Source: ICPSR 9317, FY1996.
Mean: 54.4; median: 60

Table D.4: Total Statutory Drug Minimum
Applicable in Months, 2006

Months	Frequency	Percent	Cum Percent
0	1384	45.4	45.4
3	1	.0	45.4
12	33	1.1	46.5
60	680	22.3	68.8
120	905	29.7	98.5
240	43	1.4	99.9
Life imprisonment	4	.1	100
Total	**3050**	**100**	

Source: ICPSR 20120, FY2006.
Mean: 65.6; median: 60.0

Table D.5 Mandatory Minimum Sentences by Prison In/Out for Women who Were Convicted of Drug Offenses Requiring Mandatory Minimum Sentences, 1996

Months Row pct Col. pct	Prison		Row totals
	No prison	Prison	
1	0 0% 0%	2 100.0% .2%	2 .2%
12	2 20.0% 2.2%	8 80.0% .7%	10 .9%
36	1 100.0% 1.1%	0 .0% .0%	1 .1%
60	64 11.5% 69.6%	492 88.5% 45.4%	556 47.6%
120	24 4.2% 26.1%	553 95.8% 51.1%	577 49.1%
180	1 25.0% 1.1%	3 75.0% .3%	4 .3%
240	0 0% 0%	18 100% 1.7%	18 1.5%
Life	0 .0% .0%	7 100.0% .6%	7 .6%
Column total	92 7.8%	1,083 92.2%	1,175 100.0%

Source: ICPSR 9317, FY1996.

Table D.6: Mandatory Minimum Sentences by Prison In/Out for Women who Were Convicted of Drug Offenses Requiring Mandatory Minimum Sentences, 2006

Months Row pct Col. pct	Prison		Row totals
	No prison	Prison	
3	0 .0% .0%	1 100% .1%	1 100% .1%
12	1 3% 3%	32 97% 2%	33 100% 2.0%
60	23 3.4% 69.7%	657 96.6% 40.3%	680 100% 40.9%
120	9 1% 27.3%	893 99% 54.8%	902 100% 54.2%
240	0 .0% .0%	4 100% 2.6%	43 100% 2.6%
Life	0 .0% .0%	4 100% .2%	4 100% .2%
Column total	33 2%	1630 98%	1663 100.00

Source: ICPSR 20120, FY2006.

Table D.7: Departures by Mandatory Minimum Sentences, 1996

Mandatory Minimum Sentences Attached to Offenses in Months Row pct. Column pct.	Departures				
	No departure	Upward Departure	Downward departure but no reason provided	Downward departure for substantial assistance	Totals Row # Col pct
1	2 100.0 .3				2 .2
12	5 50.0 .9			5 50.0 1.0	10 .9
36				1 100.0 .2	1 .1
60	298 54.6 51.6	2 .4 100.0	38 7.0 45.2	208 38.1 42.3	546 47.2
120	256 45.0 44.3		46 8.1 54.8	267 46.9 54.3	569 49.2
180	1 33.3 .2			2 66.7 .4	3 .3
240	13 72.2 2.2			5 27.8 1.0	18 1.6
Life	3 42.9 .5			4 57.1 .8	7 .6
Column total	578 50.0	2 .2	84 7.3	492 42.6	1,156 100.0

Source: ICPSR 9317, FY1996.

Table D.8: Departures by Mandatory Minimum Sentences, 2006

Mandatory minimum sentences attached to offenses in months Row pct. Column pct.	Departures						
	None	Upward no reason	Upward w/ *Booker*	Downward substantial assistance	Downward no reason	Downward w/*Booker*	Total
0	719 52.7% 49.9%	4 .3% 100.0%	2 .1% 40.0%	368 27.0% 34.7%	125 9.2% 53.9%	147 10.8% 54.6%	**1365** **100.0%** **45.3%**
3	1 100.0% .1%	0 .0% .0%	0 .0% .0%	0 .0% .0%	0 .0% .0%	0 .0% .0%	**1** **100.0%** **.0%**
12	22 66.7% 1.5%	0 .0% .0%	0 .0% .0%	8 24.2% .8%	1 3.0% .4%	2 6.1% .7%	**33** **100.0%** **1.1%**
60	335 49.6% 23.2%	0 .0% .0%	1 .1% 20.0%	242 35.8% 22.8%	43 6.4% 18.5%	55 8.1% 20.4%	**676** **100.0%** **22.4%**
120	346 38.8% 24.0%	0 .0% .0%	2 .2% 40.0%	416 46.6% 39.2%	63 7.1% 27.2%	65 7.3% 24.2%	**892** **100.0%** **29.6%**
240	17 40.5% 1.2%	0 .0% .0%	0 .0% .0%	25 59.5% 2.4%	0 .0% .0%	0 .0% .0%	**42** **100.0%** **1.4%**
Life	1 25.0% .1%	0 .0% .0%	0 .0% .0%	3 75.0% .3%	0 .0% .0%	0 .0% .0%	**4** **100.0%** **.1%**
Total	**1441** **47.8%** **100.0%**	**4** **.1%** **100.0%**	**5** **.2%** **100.0%**	**1062** **35.2%** **100.0%**	**232** **7.7%** **100.0%**	**269** **8.9%** **100.0%**	**3013** **100.0%** **100.0%**

Source: ICPSR 20120, FY2006.

Table D.9: Prison In/Out by Departure Status for Cases with Mandatory Minimum Sentences

Prison Count Row pct Col. pct.	Departures				Row Total
	No departure	Upward departure	Downward departure with no reason provided	Downward departure for substantial assistance	
No prison	4 4.4 .7	0 .0 .0	10 11.1 11.9	76 84.4 15.5	90 7.8
Prison	569 53.7 99.3	2 .2 100.0	74 7.0 88.1	415 39.2 84.5	1,060 92.2
Column Total	573 49.8	2 .2	84 7.3	491 42.7	1,150 100.0

Source: ICPSR 9317, FY1996.

Table D.10: Prison In/Out by Departure Status for Cases with Mandatory Minimum Sentences, 2006

Prison Count Row pct Col. pct.	Departures						
	None	Upward no reason	Upward w/*Booker*	Downward substantial assistance	Downward no reason	Downward w/*Booker*	Row Total
No prison	0 .0% .0%		0 .0% .0%	29 90.6% 4.2%	2 6.2% 1.9%	1 3.1% .8%	32 100.0% 1.9%
Prison	721 44.7% 100.0%		3 .2% 100.0%	664 41.1% 95.8%	105 6.5% 98.1%	121 7.5% 99.2%	1614 100.0% 98.1%
Column Total	721 43.8% 100.0%		3 .2% 100.0%	693 42.1% 100.0%	107 6.5% 100.0%	122 7.4% 100.0%	1646 100.0% 100.0%

Source: ICPSR 20210, FY2006.

BIBLIOGRAPHY

Adler, Freda. *Sisters in Crime*. New York, NY: McGraw Hill, 1975.

American Correctional Association. *The Female Offender: What Does the Future Hold?* Washington, DC: St. Mary's Press, 1990.

Austin, Turk. *Criminality and Legal Order*. Chicago: Rand McNally, 1969.

------------------------------. *Political Criminality: The Defiance and Defense of Authority*. Beverly Hills, CA: Sage, 1982.

Beckett, Katherine and Theodore Sasson. "The Media and the Construction of the Drug Crisis in America." *The New War on Drugs: Symbolic Politics and Criminal Justice Policy*. Ed. Eric L. Jensen and Jurg Gerber. Cincinnati, OH: ACJS/Anderson, 1998.

------------------------------. *The Politics of Injustice*. Thousand Oaks, CA: Pine Forge Press, 2000.

Belenko, Steven R. *Crack and the Evolution of Anti-drug Policy*. Westport, CT: Greenwood Press, 1993.

Bloom, Barbara, Cheoleon Lee, and Barbara Owen. "Offense Patterns Among Women Prisoners: A Preliminary Analysis." Paper presented at the *American Society of Criminology Annual Meeting*. Boston, MA, November 1995.

Bloom, Barbara and Dorothy Steinhart. *Why Punish the Children? A Reappraisal of the Children of Incarcerated Mothers in America*. San Francisco, CA: NCCD, 1993.

Bureau of Justice Statistics. BJS' Federal Justice Statistics Program Website. March 12, 2010 <http://www.fjsrc.urban.org>.

------------------------------. *Prisoners in 2007.* Washington, DC: U.S. Department of Justice, 2008.

------------------------------. *Correctional Populations in the United States, 1996.* Washington, DC: U.S. Department of Justice, 1999.

------------------------------. *Prisoners in 1998.* Washington, DC: U.S. Department of Justice, 1999.

------------------------------. *Correctional Populations in the United States, 1995.* Washington, DC: U.S. Department of Justice, 1997.

------------------------------. *Correctional Populations in the United States, 1993.* Washington, DC: U.S. Department of Justice, 1995.

------------------------------. *Women in Prison.* Washington, DC: U.S. Department of Justice, 1994.

------------------------------. *Compendium.* Washington, DC: U.S. Department of Justice, 1993.

------------------------------. *Special Report on Women in Prison.* Washington, DC: U.S. Department of Justice, 1991.

Bush-Baskette, Stephanie R. "The War on Drugs as a War against Black Women." *Crime Control and Women: Feminist Implications of Criminal Justice.* Ed. Susan L. Miller. Thousand Oaks, CA: Sage Publications, 1998: 113–129.

Caiazza, Amy, April Shaw, and Misha Werschkul. *Women's Economic Status in the States: Wide Disparities by Race, Ethnicity, and Region.* April 2004. Institute for Women's Policy Research. August 2008. <http://www.iwpr.org>

Carrington, Kerry. "Postmodernism and Feminist Criminologies: Disconnecting Discourses?" *Criminology at the Crossroads: Feminist Readings in Crime and Justice.* Ed. Kathleen Daly and Lisa Maher. New York, NY: Oxford University Press, 1998: 69–86.

Chambliss, William. "Crime Control and Ethnic Minorities: Legitimizing Racial Oppression by Creating Moral Panics." *Ethnicity, Race, and Crime: Perspectives Across Time and Place.* Ed. Darnell F. Hawkins. Albany, NY: SUNY, 1995.

Chambliss, William and Robert Seidman. *Law, Order, and Power.* Reading, MA: Addison-Wesley Publishing Co., 1971.

Chambliss, William. *Crime and the Legal Process*. New York, NY: McGraw-Hill, 1969.

Chesney-Lind, Meda. "Rethinking Women's Imprisonment: A Critical Examination of Trends in Female Incarceration." *The Criminal Justice System and Women*. Ed. Barbara Raffel Price and Natalie J. Skoloff. New York, NY: McGraw-Hill, 1995.

Daly, Kathleen. "Structure and Practice of Familial-based Justice in the Criminal Court." *Law and Society Review* 21.2 (1987): 267–290.

----------------------------------. "Neither Conflict nor Labeling nor Paternalism Will Suffice: Intersections of Race, Ethnicity, Gender and Family in Criminal Court Decisions." *Crime and Delinquency* 35.1(1989): 136–168.

----------------------------------. *Gender, Crime and Punishment*. New Haven, CT: Yale University Press, 1994.

Daly, Kathleen and Lisa Maher. "Crossroads and Intersections: Building from Feminist Critique." *Criminology at the Crossroads: Feminist Readings in Crime and Justice*. Ed. Kathleen Daly and Lisa Maher. New York, NY: Oxford University Press, 1998: 1–20.

Darendorf, Ralf. *Class and Class Conflict in Industrial Society*. Stanford, CA: Stanford University Press, 1959.

Demaris, Alfred. *Logit Modeling: Practical Applications*. Newbury Park, CA: Sage Publications, 1992.

Fairchild, Erika S. and Vincent J. Webb. "Introduction: Crime, Justice, and Politics in the United States Today." *The Politics of Crime and Criminal Justice*. Ed. Erika S. Fairchild and Vincent J. Webb. Beverly Hills, CA: Sage Publications, 1985.

Feinman, Clarice. *Women in the Criminal Justice System*. Westport, CT: Praeger, 1994.

Flanders, Laura. "Locked-Up Woman Locked Out of Coverage." *Extra!* Fairness & Accuracy In Reporting. FAIR May/June 1994. August 8, 2008. <http://www.fair.org/index.php?page=1231>

Florida Department of Corrections. *1993–94 Annual Report: The Guidebook to Corrections in Florida*. Tallahassee, FL: State of Florida, 1993/94.

----------------------------------. *Florida Department of Corrections Annual Report: Corrections as a Business*. Tallahassee, FL: State of Florida. 1994/95.

Foley, Linda A. and Christine E. Rasche. "The Effect of Race on Sentence, Actual Time Served and Final Disposition of Female Offenders." *Theory and Research in Criminal Justice*. Ed. John A. Conley. Cincinnati, OH: Anderson, 1979.

Gilbert, Nigel. *Analyzing Tabular Data*. London: UCL Press, 1993.

Glick, Ruth and Virginia Neto. *National Study of Women's Correctional Programs*. Washington, DC: National Institute of Law Enforcement and Criminal Justice, 1977.

Gutman, Herbert G. *The Black Family in Slavery and Freedom, 1750–1925*. New York, NY: Vintage Books, 1976.

Hagan, John. "Toward a Structural Theory of Crime, Race, and Gender: The Canadian Case." *Crime and Delinquency* 3.1(1985): 129–146.

Harris, Angela. "Race and Essentialism in Feminist Legal Theory." *Critical Race Feminism*. Ed. Adrien Katherine Wing. New York: New York University Press, 1997.

Harris, A.P. "Race and Essentialism in Feminist Legal Theory." *Stanford Legal Review* 42 (1990): 581–616.

Hooks, Bell. *Ain't I A Woman*. Boston, MA: South End Press, 1981.

----------------------------------. *Feminist Theory from Margin to Center*. Boston, MA: South End Press, 1984.

----------------------------------. *Killing Rage*. New York: Henry Holt and Company, 1997.

Horowitz, Craig. "The No-Win War." *New York Magazine*. 5 Feb. 1996: 22–33.

Huling, Tracy. "Prisoners of War: Woman Drug Couriers in the United States." *Drug Couriers: A New Perspective*. Ed. Martin D. Schwartz and Dragan Milovanovic. London: Quartet Books Unlimited, 1996.

Human Rights 95. Alfreda Robinson, Drug War POW. November 27, 2009. <http://wwwhr95.org/robinson,a.htm>

Humphries, Drew. *Crack Mothers*. OH: Ohio State University Press, 1999.

----------------------------------. "Crack Mothers at 6: Prime-Time News, Crack/Cocaine, and Women." *Violence Against Women* 4.1 (1998): 45-61.

Inciardi, James A., Dorothy Lockwood, and Anne E. Pottieger. *Women and Crack-Cocaine*. NY: Macmillan Publishing, 1993.

Jacobs, Harriet A. *Incidents in the Life of a Slave Girl Written by Herself.* Cambridge, MA: Harvard University Press, 1987.

Jensen, Eric and Jurg Gerber. "The Social Construction of Drug Problems: An Historical Overview." *The New War on Drugs: Symbolic Politics and Criminal Justice Policy.* Ed. Eric L. Jensen and Jurg Gerber. Cincinnati, OH: ACJS/Anderson, 1998.

Kline, Sue. "A Profile of Female Offenders in State and Federal Prisons." *Female Offenders: Meeting Needs of a Neglected Population.* Baltimore, MD: United Book Press, 1993.

Kruttschnitt, Candace. "Social Status and Sentences of Female Offenders." *Law and Society* 15.2(1980–1981): 247–265.

Langdon, Neal P. and Bernadette Pelissier. "Gender Differences Among Prisoners in Drug Treatment." Federal Bureau of Prisons, 2001. May 12, 2008. <http://www.bop.gov/news/reserach_reports.jsp#drug>

Lewis, Diane. "Black Women Offenders and Criminal Justice." *Comparing Female and Male Offenders. Ed.* Marguerite Q. Warren. Newbury Park, CA: Sage Publications, 1981. 89–105.

Lewis–Beck, Michael. *Applied Regression.* Thousand Oaks, CA: Sage Publications, 1980.

Lilly, J. Robert, Francis T. Cullen, and Richard A. Ball. *Criminological Theory: Context and Consequences.* Thousand Oaks, CA: Sage Publications, 1995.

Maguire, Kathleen and Ann L. Pastore. *Sourcebook of Criminal Justice Statistics.* Bureau of Justice Statistics. Washington, DC: U.S. Department of Justice, 1998.

Maher, Lisa. *Sexed Work.* Oxford: Clarendon Press, 1997.

Mann, Cora Mae Richey. "Minority and Female: A Criminal Justice Double Bind." *Social Justice* 16.4(1989.): 95.

--------------------------------. *Unequal Justice: A Question of Color.* Bloomington, IN: Indiana University, 1993.

--------------------------------. "Women of Color and the Criminal Justice System." *The Criminal Justice System and Women.* Ed. Barbara Raffel Price and Natalie J. Skoloff. New York, NY: McGraw-Hill, 1995.

Maxfield, Linda D. and John H. Kramer. *Substantial Assistance: An Empirical Yardstick Gauging Equity in Current Federal Policy and Practice.* United

States Sentencing Commission. Washington, DC: U.S. Government Printing Office, 1998.

Mauer, Mark and Tracey Huling. *Young Black Americans and the Criminal Justice System: Five Years Later.* Washington, DC: The Sentencing Project, 1995.

Menard, Scott. *Applied Logistic Regression Analysis.* Thousand Oaks, CA: Sage Publications, 1995.

Miller, Jerome G. *Search and Destroy: African-American Males in the Criminal Justice System.* Boston, MA: Cambridge University Press, 1996.

Miller, Marc and Ronald Wright. "Your Cheatin' Heart(land): The Long Search for Administrative Sentencing Justice." *Buffalo Criminal Law Review* 2.2 (1999): 723–813.

Morgan, John P. and Lynn Zimmer. "The Social Pharmacology of Smokeable Cocaine." *Crack in America.* Ed. Craig Reinarman and Henry Levine. Berkeley: University Press, 1997.

Mumola, Christopher J. and Jennifer C. Karberg. *Drug Use and Dependence, State and Federal Prisoners.* Bureau of Justice Statistics. Washington, DC: U.S. Department of Justice, 2007.

National Drug Control Strategy. *FY 2001 Budget Summary.* Office of the National Drug Control Policy, 2000.

National Council on Crime and Delinquency. *National Drug Statement.* Hackensack, NJ: NCCD, 1991.

National Institute of Justice. *2000 Arrestee: Drug Abuse Monitoring: Annual Report.* Washington, DC: U.S. Department of Justice, April 2003.

Norusis, Marija. *SPSS for Windows, Base System User's Guide, Release 6.0.* Chicago, IL: SPSS, 1993.

November Coalition. 2009. The Wall Women and the Drug War. http:/November.org/thewall/cases/clark-c/clark-c.html. 11/27/2009

-------------------------- <http://november.org/thewall/cases/cunningham-m/cunningham-m.html. 11/27/2009.>

-------------------------- <http://www/hr95.org/Drake,T.html. 11/27/2009.>

---------------------------------- <http://november.org/thewall/cases/hasan-h/hasan-h.html. 11/27/2009>

---------------------------------- <http://November.org/thewall/cases/metz-d/metz-d.html. 11/27/2009>

---------------------------------- <http://November.org/thewall/cases/nod-s/ nod-s.html. 11/27/2009.>

---------------------------------- <http:/November.org/thewall/cases/wade-v/ wade-v.html. 11/27/2009>

Odubekon, Lola. "A Structural Approach to Differential Gender Sentencing." *Criminal Justice Abstracts* 2 (1992): 343–60.

Omole, Omolola E. *Clarifying the Role of Gender in the Court Dispositions: A LISREL Model of Pretrial Release*. Michigan: UMI, 1991.

Ortiz, Vilma. "Women of Color: A Demographic Overview." *Women of Color in U.S. Society*. Ed. Maxine Baca Zinn and Bonnie Thornton Dill. Philadelphia, PA: Temple University Press, 1994.

Paige M. Harrison and Allen J. Beck. *Prisoners in 2004*. Bureau of Justice Statistics. Washington, DC: Department of Justice, 2005.

Rafter, Nicole Hahn. *Partial Justice: Women, Prisons and Social Control*. New Brunswick, NJ: Transaction Books, 1990.

Rasmussen, David W. and Bruce L. Benson. *The Economic Anatomy of a Drug War*. Lanham, MD: Rowman and Littlefield Publishers, Inc., 1994.

Reinarman, Craig and Henry Levine. "Crack in Context: Politics and Media in the Making of a Drug Scare." *Contemporary Drug Problems* 16.4(1989): 535–577.

---------------------------------. "The Crack Attack: Politics and Media in America's Latest Drug Scare." *Images of Issues*. Ed. Joel Best. New York, NY: Aldine De Gruyter, 1990.

---------------------------------. "Crack in Context: America's Latest Demon Drug." *Crack in America*. Ed. Craig Reinarman and Henry Levine. Berkeley: University Press, 1997.

---------------------------------. "The Crack Attack: Politics and the Media in the Crack Scare." *Crack in America*. Ed. Craig Reinarman and Henry Levine. Berkeley, CA: University Press, 1997.

Rice, Marcia. "Challenging Orthodoxies in Feminist Theory: A Black Feminist Critique." *Feminist Perspectives in Criminology*. Ed. Loraine Gelsthorpe and Allison Morris. Bristol, PA: Open University Press, 1992.

Scheingold, Stuart A. *The Politics of Law and Order: Street Crime and Public Policy*. New York, NY: Longman, 1984.

Simpson, Sally. "Feminist Theory, Crime, and Justice." *Criminology* 27.4 (1989): 605–631.

Simon, Rita and Jean Landis. *The Crimes Women Commit and the Punishments They Receive.* Lexington, MA: Lexington Books, 1991.

Spohn, Cassia, John Gruhl, and Susan Welch. "The Impact of the Ethnicity and Gender of Defendants on the Decision to Reject or Dismiss Felony Charges." *Criminology* 25.1(1987): 175–191.

Stenson, Kevin. "Making Sense of Crime Control." *The Politics of Crime Control.* Ed. Kevin Stenson and David Cowell. Newbury Park: Sage Publications, 1991.

Tonry, Michael. *Malign Neglect.* New York, NY: Oxford University Press, 1995.

United States Department of Commerce, Bureau of the Census, 2005 American Community Survey, calculated by the Institute for Women's Policy Research.

U.S. Department of Health and Human Services, Health Resources and Services Administration. *Women's Health USA 2006.* Rockville, Maryland: U.S. Department of Health and Human Services, 2006.

United States Sentencing Commission. *Report to the Congress: Cocaine and Federal Sentencing Policy.* Washington, DC: U.S. Government Printing Office, 2007.

--------------------------------. *Sourcebook of Federal Sentencing Statistics.* 2004. May 15, 2006. <http://www.ussc.gov/ANNRPT/2004/ar04toc.htm>

--------------------------------. *Fifteen Years of Guidelines Sentencing.* Washington, DC: U.S. Government Printing Office, 2004.

--------------------------------. *Sourcebook of Federal Sentencing Statistics.* Washington, DC: US Government Printing Office, 2002.

--------------------------------. *Special Report to the Congress: Cocaine and Federal Sentencing Policy.* Washington, DC: US Government Printing Office, 1997.

--------------------------------. *Special Report to the Congress: Cocaine and Federal Sentencing Policy.* Washington, DC: US Government Printing Office, 1995.

--------------------------------. *Special Report to the Congress: Mandatory Minimum Penalties in the Federal Criminal Justice System.* Washington, DC: U.S. Government Printing Office, 1991.

United States Department of Justice. *Federal Criminal Case Processing, 1982–1993*. Washington, DC: U.S. Government Printing Office, 1996.

Visher, Christy. "Gender, Police Arrest Decisions, and Notions of Chivalry." *Criminology* 21.1 (1983): 5–28.

Vold, George. *Theoretical Criminology*. New York, NY: Oxford University Press, 1958.

Webb, Gary L. and Michel P. Brown. "United States Drug Laws and Institutionalized Discrimination." *The New War on Drugs: Symbolic Politics and Criminal Justice Policy*. Ed. Eric L. Jensen and Jurg Gerber. Cincinnati, OH: ACJS/Anderson, 1998.

Webster. *Merriam-Webster's Collegiate Dictionary*. Springfield, MA: Merriam-Webster Inc., 1993.

Weisburd, David, Stanton Wheeler, Elin Waring, and Nancy Bode. *Crimes of the Middle Class*. New Haven, CT: Yale University Press, 1991.

Wing, Adrien K. "Essentialism and Anti-Essentialism: Ain't I a Woman?" *Critical Race Feminism*. Ed. Adrien K. Wing. New York, NY: New York University, 1997.

Young, Vernetta. "Gender Expectations and Their Impact on Black Female Offenders and Their Victims." *Justice Quarterly* 3.2(1986): 305–327.

— Statutes

21 USC 13 (I) (D) 841
21 USC 13 (I) (D) 844
21 USC 13 (1)(D) 846

— Cases

Booker v. United States 543 U.S. 220 (2005)
Pinkerton v. United States, 328 U.S. 640 (1946)

INDEX

171

black males, rates of, 111
females, rates of, 22, 117, 118
and political resistance, 129
rates of, by demographics, 15, 16,
17, 31
urban inhabitants, rates of, 121
ASFA (Adoption and Safe Families Act),
132

B

barbiturates, 48
base form of cocaine, 26, 36, 48
base offense levels, 40, 41
Bennett, William, 32
Benson, Bruce L., 32, 168
benzocaine, 48
Bias, Len, 34
Biden, Joseph, 135
black, defined, 14n35
black females
and anti-essentialism, 109–112
convictions of, 65, 80, 96
and crack cocaine, 66, 80, 85,
107, 121
and disparity. *See* disparity
and disproportionality. *See*
disproportionality
marginalized status of, 112–115,
118, 127
media portrayal of, 35, 36, 107
as "others," 36, 108, 118
research results on, 88–98, 121–
125, 136–139
research statistics on, 62–66, 67t,
68t, 69t, 70–74, 75t, 76t, 77,
80, 81, 82, 83, 85, 86
social costs of drug policies on,
125–127
status of, 107. *See also* black
females, marginalized status of;
lower class
as targets/victims of war on drugs,

98, 100, 107, 108, 130, 138
black males, 2, 3, 3t, 10, 17, 110,
113, 114, 118, 119, 138
Blakely v. Washington, 46
bureaucratic organizations
agendas of, 105–106
strain on, 106
burglary, 20, 117

C

caffeine, 48
Caiazza, Amy, 115, 163
California
as destination for powdered
cocaine shipments, 47
sentencing outcomes for females
in, 117
study of jailed females in, 116,
117
and U.S. female prison
population, 55
Caribbean nations, as source of
powdered cocaine, 47
Chambliss, William, 6, 101, 103,
107, 128, 163, 164
children
of incarcerated women, 110, 132
prenatal exposure to drugs, 133
cigarettes, cocaine as ingredient in,
47
cigars, cocaine as ingredient in, 47
city. *See also* inner city
drug sales in, 47
media representation of, 107
policing tactics in, 106, 121, 128
stigmatization in, 19
class-based society, and treatment by
criminal justice system, 106
Clinton, Bill, 30, 37, 128
Coca-Cola, cocaine as ingredient in,
47

LaVergne, TN USA
17 September 2010
197480LV00002B/48/P

NOV 0 1 2010